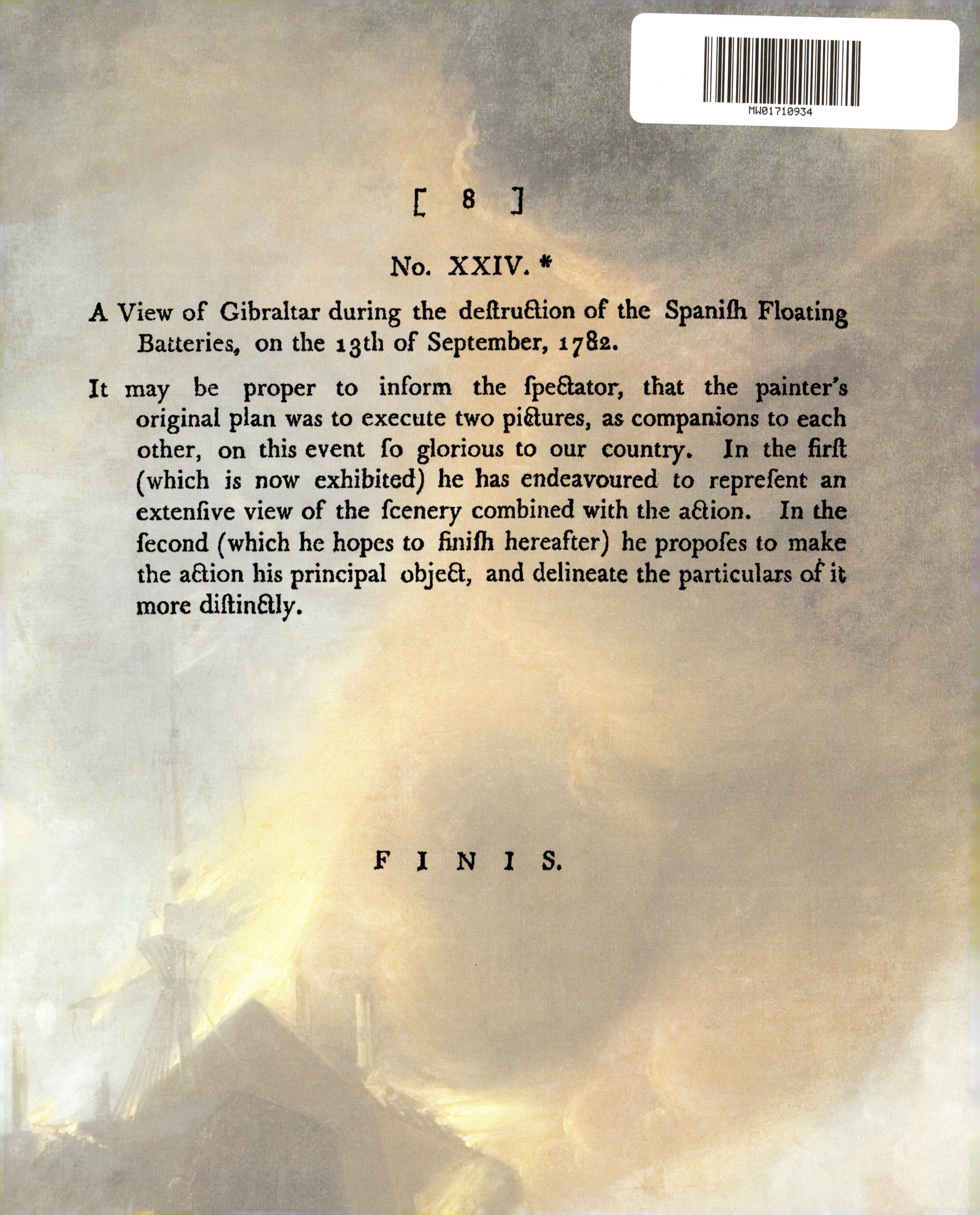

No. XXIV. *

A View of Gibraltar during the deſtruction of the Spaniſh Floating Batteries, on the 13th of September, 1782.

It may be proper to inform the ſpectator, that the painter's original plan was to execute two pictures, as companions to each other, on this event ſo glorious to our country. In the firſt (which is now exhibited) he has endeavoured to repreſent an extenſive view of the ſcenery combined with the action. In the ſecond (which he hopes to finiſh hereafter) he propoſes to make the action his principal object, and delineate the particulars of it more diſtinctly.

F I N I S.

LOST AND FOUND

WRIGHT OF DERBY'S *VIEW OF GIBRALTAR*

LOST AND FOUND

WRIGHT OF DERBY'S *VIEW OF GIBRALTAR*

ESSAYS BY

JOHN BONEHILL

JANET M. BROOKE

BARBARA KLEMPAN

DAVID DE WITT

AGNES ETHERINGTON ART CENTRE,

QUEEN'S UNIVERSITY, KINGSTON, CANADA

Published on the occasion of the exhibition *Lost and Found: Wright of Derby's View of Gibraltar,* presented at the Agnes Etherington Art Centre, Queen's University, Kingston ON, Canada from 5 February to 12 June 2011.

The Agnes Etherington Art Centre gratefully acknowledges the support of The Paul Mellon Centre for Studies in British Art, and of Alfred and Isabel Bader in the production of this publication.

Organizers: Janet M. Brooke, Director
David de Witt, Bader Curator of European Art

Authors: John Bonehill, Lecturer, History of Art, University of Glasgow
Janet M. Brooke
Barbara Klempan, Associate Professor, Master of Art Conservation, Queen's University, Kingston
David de Witt

Publication management: Janet M. Brooke

Editor: Shannon Anderson

Design: Associés libres, Montréal

Printing: Marquis Book Printing Inc.

Distribution: ABC Art Books Canada/ABC Livres d'art Canada
www.abcartbookscanada.com

Agnes Etherington Art Centre
Queen's University
Kingston ON, Canada K7L 3N6
www.aeac.ca

Library and Archives Canada Cataloguing in Publication

Lost and found : Wright of Derby's View of Gibraltar / essays by John Bonehill, Janet M. Brooke, Barbara Klempan, David de Witt.

ISBN 978-1-55339-258-3

1. Wright, Joseph, 1734-1797. A View of Gibraltar. 2. History painting--Ontario--Kingston. 3. Agnes Etherington Art Centre. I. Wright, Joseph, 1734-1797 II. Bonehill, John III. Brooke, Janet M. IV. Klempan, Barbara V. De Witt, David VI. Agnes Etherington Art Centre VII. Title: Lost and Found: Wright of Derby's View of Gibraltar.

ND497.W8A75 2011 759.2 C2010-907961-2

Every reasonable attempt has been made to identify owners of copyright. Errors or omissions will be corrected in subsequent reprints.

Endpapers: cat. 1 (details, digitally altered); citation from *A Catalogue of Pictures, Painted by J. Wright, of Derby, and Exhibited at Mr. Robins's Rooms...* (London: J. Barker, 1785), p. 8, no. 24.

ONTARIO ARTS COUNCIL
CONSEIL DES ARTS DE L'ONTARIO

CONTENTS

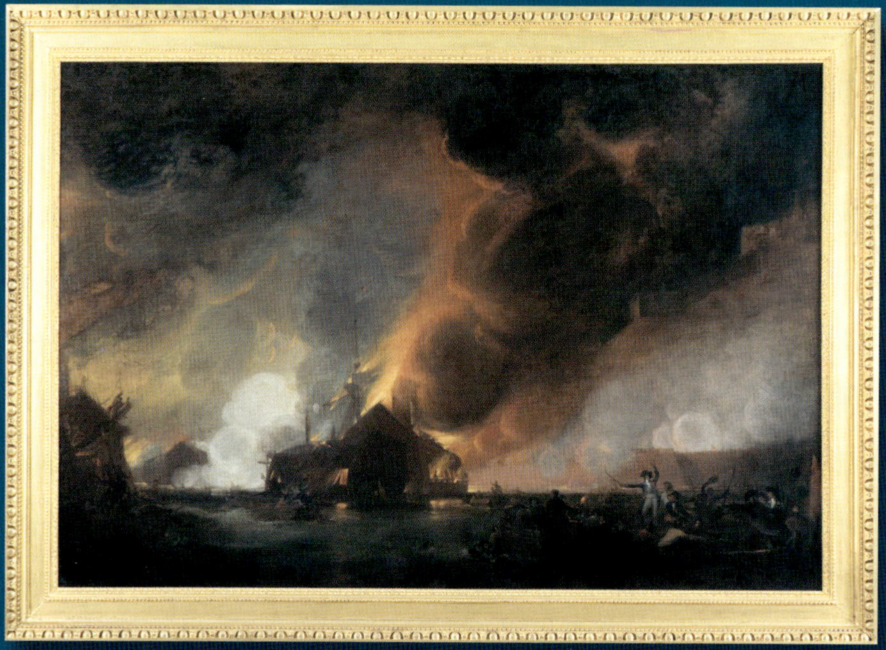

Cat. 1.
Joseph Wright of Derby
A View of Gibraltar during the destruction of the Spanish Floating Batteries, on the 13th of September, 1782

1785
Oil on canvas
160.9 × 234.7 cm

PREFACE

SINCE ITS ACQUISITION in 2001, *A View of Gibraltar during the destruction of the Spanish Floating Batteries, on the 13th of September, 1782* has taken the Agnes Etherington Art Centre's European art specialists on a fascinating journey. The large painting entered our collection in poor condition, and with a complicated history of ownership and attributions. As a university art gallery with scholarly resources close to hand, the Art Centre embarked on the journey to unravel this painting's history with dedication and pleasure. In *Lost and Found: Wright of Derby's View of Gibraltar* we share its results, bringing together expertise in art history, conservation science and provenance research to affirm the attribution—hitherto long in doubt—of one of the great history paintings by the eighteenth century British artist Joseph Wright of Derby.

I salute with enthusiasm the contributions of my co-authors in this publication; our collaboration in applying various methodologies to resolve an art historical mystery has been both rewarding and fruitful. I am particularly grateful to our long-time patron Dr. Alfred Bader, who supported the Art Centre's acquisition of *A View of Gibraltar* and its laborious conservation treatment; his steadfast commitment to our research has been both inspiring and motivating. In fact, our shared interest in Wright of Derby predates this acquisition by some years: again thanks to a contribution from Dr. Bader, we acquired an extraordinary corpus of eight landscapes by the artist from a Canadian private collection in 1988. These works accompany *A View of Gibraltar* in our exhibition, and together constitute the largest holding of the artist's paintings in North America.

I also extend the Art Centre's sincere thanks to The Paul Mellon Centre for Studies in British Art for its contribution towards the publication of this catalogue. In an era when public galleries are increasingly challenged in their efforts to undertake sustained collection research and to disseminate their findings, its support has helped to ensure that Wright of Derby's *View of Gibraltar* takes its rightful place in the artist's canon.

Janet M. Brooke
Director

ABBREVIATED LITERATURE

Barker 2009
Elizabeth Barker. "Documents Relating to Joseph Wright 'of Derby' (1734–97)." *The Walpole Society* 71 (2009), pp. 1–216.

Bemrose 1885
William Bemrose. *The Life and Works of Joseph Wright of Derby, A.R.A., commonly called "Wright of Derby."* London: Bemrose and Sons, 1885.

Bonehill 2008
John Bonehill. "Laying Siege to the Royal Academy: Wright of Derby's *View of Gibraltar* at Robins's Rooms, Covent Garden, April 1785." *Art History* 30, no. 4 (September 2008), pp. 521–544.

Bradbury 1883
Edward Bradbury. "Wright of Derby: The Man and his Work." *Time: A Monthly Miscellany of Interesting and Amusing Literature* 8 (1883), pp. 590–600.

Egerton 1990
Judy Egerton. *Wright of Derby*. Exhibition catalogue. London: Tate Gallery; Paris: Grand Palais; and New York: Metropolitan Museum of Art, 1990.

Erdmann 1974
Biruta Erdmann. "Wright of Derby's 'The Siege of Gibraltar.'" *Burlington Magazine* 116, no. 854 (May 1974), pp. 270–272.

Hayley 1785
William Hayley. *A Catalogue of Pictures, Painted by J. Wright, of Derby, and Exhibited at Mr. Robins's Rooms under the Great Piazza, Covent Garden*. Exhibition catalogue. London: J. Barker, 1785.

Jones 1990
Rica Jones. "Wright of Derby's Techniques of Painting." In Egerton 1990, pp. 263–271.

Nicolson 1968
Benedict Nicolson. *Joseph Wright of Derby, Painter of Light*. Studies in British Art. 2 vols. London: Routledge and Kegan Paul; and New York: Pantheon Books, for The Paul Mellon Foundation for British Art, 1968.

Nicolson 1988
Benedict Nicolson. "Wright of Derby: Addenda and Corrigenda." *Burlington Magazine* 130, no. 1027 (October 1988), pp. 745–758.

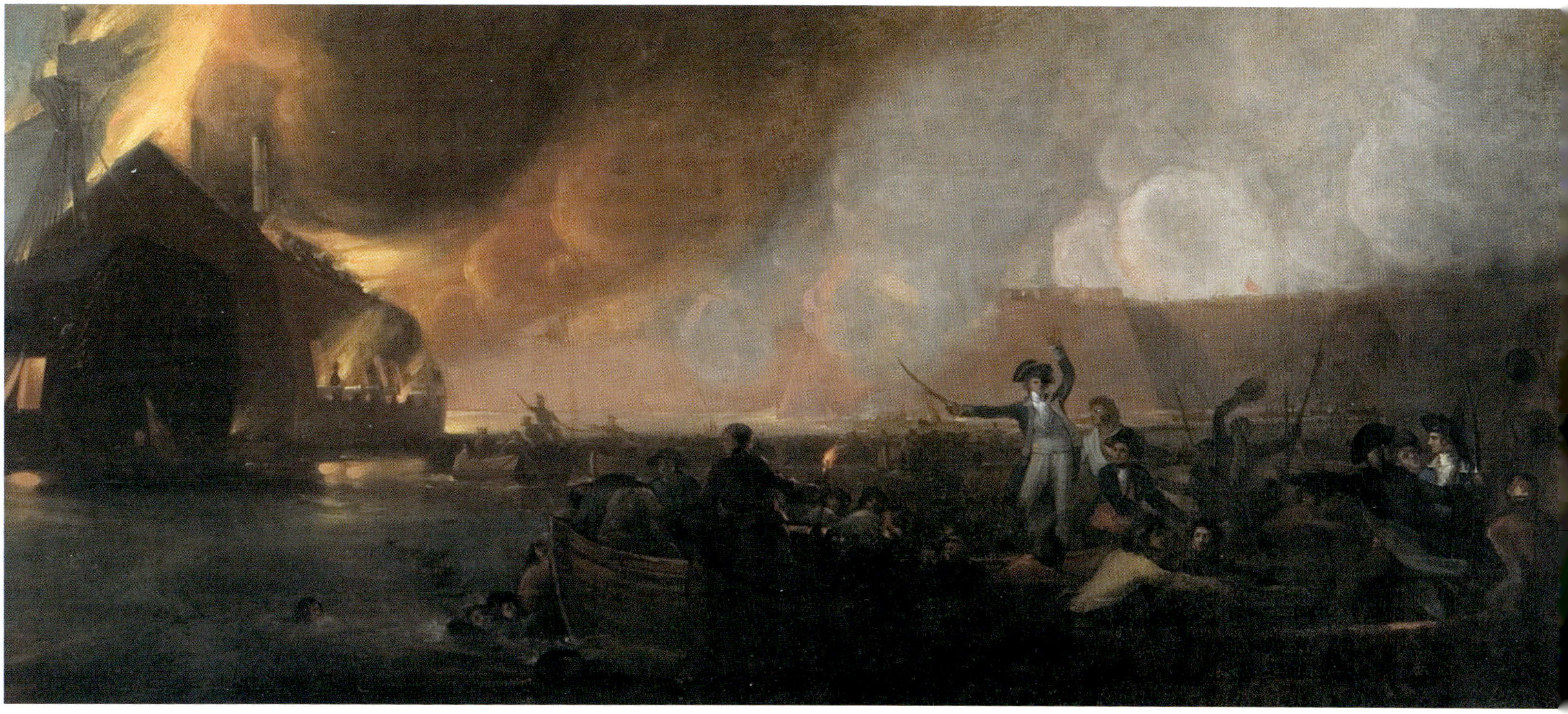

"ARTIST AND BARD IN SWEET ALLIANCE": JOSEPH WRIGHT OF DERBY'S SOCIAL CIRCLES AND THE MAKING OF *A VIEW OF GIBRALTAR*

JOHN BONEHILL

IN A LETTER to the poet William Hayley (1745–1820), dated 13 January 1783, Joseph Wright began to outline his plans for a painted tribute to the defenders of the garrison of Gibraltar, who had lately emerged victorious from a Franco-Spanish siege lasting some three years. "Ever since I read in the Papers the account of the late great Event of Gibrates I have been fired wth a Desire of bringing so great an effect on Canvass," observed the painter.[1] Over the next two years Wright exchanged numerous letters with his correspondent updating him on the slow progress of his epic painting as well as the planning and staging of its first public display, as the centrepiece of a pioneering one-man show at Robins's Rooms, Covent Garden, in April 1785. Hayley not only orchestrated the iconography of the exhibition but also prepared the ground for its reception in a series of verses and reports planted in the press. This essay will explore this collaboration of painter and poet as well as the roles others in their social circle played in the making of Wright's *A View of Gibraltar during the destruction of the Spanish Floating Batteries, on the 13th of September, 1782* and related plans for its highly theatrical and politically charged exhibition.

On the evidence of his correspondence Wright was chimerical, often swayed by the desire to please friends who gave him diverse, oftentimes contradictory advice. Far from the robust midlands "man of reason" familiar from much of the literature on the artist, Wright was a figure who looked to long-term friends, patrons or well-known men of letters, for authority in matters artistic. The famous "variety" of his work, so much commented upon by his contemporaries, was, in some respects, a consequence of the shifts in his company and the desire to impress his various more intellectually confident associates. Wright's short-term interest in natural philosophy, as it found expression in paintings such as *A Philosopher giving that lecture on the Orrery, in which a Lamp is put in place of the Sun*,[2] exhibited in 1766, entirely coincided with, and was a product of his association with the cartographer, engineer and printmaker Peter Perez Burdett (1734/35–1793). The painter altered the course of his work, abandoning this type of subject, after his friend left Derbyshire and him. Wright frequently painted subjects that his friends advised, most of the subjects featured in the exhibition of 1785 being dictated by Hayley or mutual friends such as the physician William Long (1747–1818). In the final years of his life, Wright received support from a new social circle led by much younger men, including the cleric Thomas Gisborne (1758–1846) and the entrepreneurs, John Leigh Philips (1761–1814) and Thomas Moss Tate (d. 1825). These men, his confidantes and constant correspondents, saw him differently from earlier friends and patrons and promoted a fresh phase of Wright's art, much redolent of private and melancholy encounter with the landscapes of the midlands or the Lake District. Thus, it is possible to understand Wright's œuvre as testimony to shifting and diverse social circles, often held apart by the artist, to a series of collaborations with friends who were also advisers, agents, publicists and patrons of his art.

I.

In 1778, Wright made his debut at the Royal Academy, having defected from the then failing rival Society of Artists. Wright submitted pictures that extended his subject matter, introducing dramatic, nocturnal views of the Italian landscape, urban and rural, illuminated by fireworks or volcanic turbulence, along with atmospheric scenes of underground grottos and caverns, as well as paintings of subjects derived from the contemporary literature of sensibility, such as James Beattie's *Minstrel* and Lawrence Sterne's *A Sentimental Journey*. Wright's versatility prompted the critic of the *Morning Chronicle* to observe, "his *forte* is peculiar to himself, and is not more singular to himself," finding each exhibit "materially differing from the other in point of excellence."[3] Hayley's first major publication, *An Epistle to an Eminent Painter* (or *An Essay on Painting*), a poetic history of the art, consisting of two lengthy, comparative verses, the first recording the achievements of antiquity, together with painting's subsequent decline and eventual rebirth in Italy, and the second celebrating the triumphs of contemporary British art, appeared the same year, and contained lines further promoting Wright's "singularity":

> See far off the modest WRIGHT retire!
> Alone he rules his Element of Fire:
> Like Meteors darting through the gloom of Night,
> His sparkles flash upon the dazzled fight.[4]

Wright's friendship with Hayley appears to have began in earnest around this time, and can be traced together with their subsequent artistic collaboration through surviving correspondence. "It is recommended to the Painters, who wish to become eminent to let no day pass without a line," Wright observed of their relationship.[5] In the epistolary style of polite society, the artist's letters to and those received from his literary mentor frequently shift between the personal and the professional, from easy discussion of mutual acquaintances to debate over iconographic meaning, from complaints of the painter's disabling bouts of melancholy to a keen concern for the marketing of his works.[6] In the wake of the success of Hayley's signature work, the long, didactic poem *The Triumphs of Temper*, written and published in 1781, the association was of some advantage to the artist, especially as he sought to fashion himself a literary painter, the poet suggesting subjects and, from what little evidence we have of Wright's library, his reading, furnishing the artist with copies of his own works and those of his friends such as John Sargent.[7] This is not to deny, however, the poet's own enthusiastic promotion of their relationship, or the capital to be accrued from such a connection on his part. This became an increasingly important bond once Wright's relationship with the Academy foundered.

Although Wright had been elected an Associate Academician as early as November 1781, he was to be defeated by one Edmund Garvey (1740–1813) when a full membership became available in February 1783.[8] Garvey's preferment occasioned a good deal of speculation among contemporaries, who were largely mystified by the decision to promote a patent nonentity ahead of the distinguished Wright. In his 1786 dramatic satire, *The Royal Academicians, A Farce*, John Williams (1754–1818), writing as Anthony Pasquin, observed that: "the inimitable *Wright* of Derby *once* expressed an ardent desire to be a member of the Academy; but from what unaccountable reason his wishes were frustrated remains as yet a secret to the world; but the sagacious or rather *envious* brethren of the Brush thought proper to *thrust* so eminent an artist to one side, to make way for the admission of so contemptible an animal as *Edmund Garbage*."[9] Williams's reading of the situation was, no doubt, shaped by a number of publications that appeared in the wake of the incident, commencing with Hayley's *Ode to Mr. Wright of Derby*, "distributed, without regular publication" in the summer of 1783.[10] This lengthy verse tribute was clearly prompted by the artist's breaking with the Academy earlier that year, and related plans to paint a large, ambitious canvas celebrating the successful defence of Gibraltar. Hayley's lines call on the Derby painter to "Give to our view our favourite scenes of Fame, / Where Britain's Genius blaz'd in glory's brightest flame," to celebrate the glorious victory at Gibraltar in paint:

> Proud Calpe bids thee, Wright, display
> The terrors of her blazing rock:
> The burning bulks of baffled Spain,
> From thee she claims, nor claims in vain,
> Thou mighty master of the mimic flame,
> Whose peerless pencil, with peculiar aim,
> Has form'd of lasting fire the basis of thy fame.[11]

Hayley's verse celebrates the triumph of British arms as likely to promote a national art, with Wright the patriot artist best able to capitalize on this opportunity for a civic-minded painting. Wright's dedication to his art is then contrasted with the practice of figures prominent in the politics of the London art establishment, who make up "dark cabals" and whose "base intrigues / Exclude meek Merit from his proper home." He was to find support in Hayley, another modest and refined artistic personality, removed from the world: "Artist and Bard in sweet alliance; / They suffer equal wounds, and mutual aid demand."[12] In reply, Wright was moved to thank the poet for "your very spirited Ode wch breathes so much fire & friendship."[13]

II.

When first alerting Hayley to his plans to commemorate recent events in the Mediterranean in paint in his letter of mid-January 1783, Wright cautioned that the subject was "already in the hands of several & will soon be a Hackney'd one." Indeed, Hayley's subsequent verse was prompted as much by his friend's break with the Academy as by the appearance of several rival versions of the siege at that year's Academy exhibition, pictures that prompted one critic to complain of his patience being "literally worn out with looking at floating batteries and Gibraltar."[14] Artists were attracted by the opportunity to display their handling of dramatic, sublime effects as well as a narrative that pitted British fellow feeling against the callous indifference of the enemy, where regard for others might be represented as a characteristic national trait. After more than three years of siege warfare the Bourbon blockade had come to an end following a climactic battle waged over the night of 13–14 September 1782. In an attempt to enforce the final submission of the garrison, the allies amassed a line of battering ships intended to breach fortress defences. These floating batteries were to succumb to a constant rain of red-hot shot from the defenders, however. Cannon fire struck the magazines of the ships and they exploded, leaving the crews in what contemporaries reported as "deepest Distress, and all imploring Assistance," forming "a Spectacle of Horror not easily to be described."[15] Abandoned by their own leadership, the drowning were rescued by Captain Roger Curtis (1746–1816) on order of his garrison commander General George Augustus Elliot (1717–1790). On hearing of the victory, Horace Walpole (1717–1797), writing to William Wentworth, Earl of Stafford (1722–1791), was led to comment: "At this moment if I was an epicure among the sharks, I should rejoice that General Elliott has just sent the carcasses of 1500 Spaniards down the market under Gibraltar – but I am more pleased that he despatched boats and saved some of those whom he had overset. What must a man of so much feeling have suffered at being forced to do his duty so well as he had done!"[16] This image of Elliot as a representative "man of feeling" was endorsed across any number of verse tributes and commemorative prints rushed out in the aftermath of the defence of the Rock, in ways that accorded with contemporary models of moral rectitude and heroism. In his 1778 *Essays, Moral and Literary*, Vicesimus Knox (1752–1821) observed: "The greatest mildness is commonly united with the greatest fortitude, in the true hero."[17] Elliot's actions and those of men under his command were of obvious appeal to those who cultivated a reputation for feeling, such as Wright and Hayley.

Wright struggled to bring his *View of Gibraltar* to completion, delayed by bouts of ill health as well as a lack of access to appropriate documentary sources. Despite Hayley's best efforts to establish contact with veterans of the siege, who collaborated with a number of Wright's rivals, he was unable to gain the Derby painter access. Following procedures pioneered in the portrayal of contemporary histories by John Singleton Copley (1738–1815), who was himself engaged in painting the siege, artists of the period sought to assert the accuracy, what Wright termed the "historical truth," of their design, whether by reference to documentary evidence or collusion with an eye-witness.[18] Such was Wright's concern to ensure a degree of fidelity to events on the Rock he made at least two rare excursions to London, visiting the Treasury in the company of the leading natural philosopher, John Whitehurst (1713–1788), a long-time Derby associate. According to a letter of the period, Whitehurst "had got sight often of a dozen Drawings of Gibraltar, one of wch represented the Action." Although the painter was unable to see this particular work when in London, he was still able to copy "two of the Drawings for the sake of the scenery wch is grand indeed, independent of the Action, & if I should paint two pictures it will do admirably for that, in wch the scenery shall be principal, the Action subservient, & make a good Companion to the other, where the action will be principal."[19] It appears that Wright always intended to execute two pictures of the siege, as is further indicated by a letter to Hayley, which also announced his completion of the painting and provides the fullest contemporary description of the picture:

> After all I fear it is not the picture you expect to see, as the action is not principal and at too great a distance to discriminate particulars, even the men in the Gunboats that lie off the New Mole (wch makes a fine dark foreground to the picture) are not more than an inch high. However the floating batteries in different degrees of burning make a fine blaze and illuminate in a striking manner the noble Rock of Gib.[20]

A View of Gibraltar as exhibited in 1785 was not the picture Wright had originally planned and which Hayley had trumpeted in the *Ode*, where the action would "be principal." Nevertheless, it made a startling showing when viewed alongside other recent works in the painter's London exhibition.

III.

Over two years in preparation, *A View of Gibraltar* was puffed extensively in the lead up to its eventual showing, alongside a range of exhibits promoting the artist's varied abilities as a landscapist, portraitist and literary painter, at Robins's Rooms, Covent Garden in April 1785. A correspondent for the *General Evening Post*, writing in early January, reported how:

> On stopping at Derby, a few days since, I was introduced by a friend to view the productions of that great genius Wright, whose astonishing power of expressing artificial lights on canvas, the world has been long acquainted with. – His new picture on the siege of Gibraltar, for composition, force, brilliancy, and prodigious effect of fire, exceeds, in my opinion, all his former labours. – to attempt a description of it would be in vain; whoever sees the picture, must have such an idea of the action as no poetry can describe. – Mr. Wright has not been in the Exhibition, from reasons I cannot explain, for some time past, but that he will not withhold this sublime piece from general inspection, I most ardently hope, as the attack on Gibraltar, with some other pieces on interesting subjects, would form an exhibition every way worthy of the countenance of the public.[21]

Wright's show, centred around *A View of Gibraltar*, was conceived from the outset as linked to his recent absence from the London showrooms and, by extension, his dispute with the Academy. With the Society of Artists failing, those figures disillusioned with conditions imposed by the Royal Academy

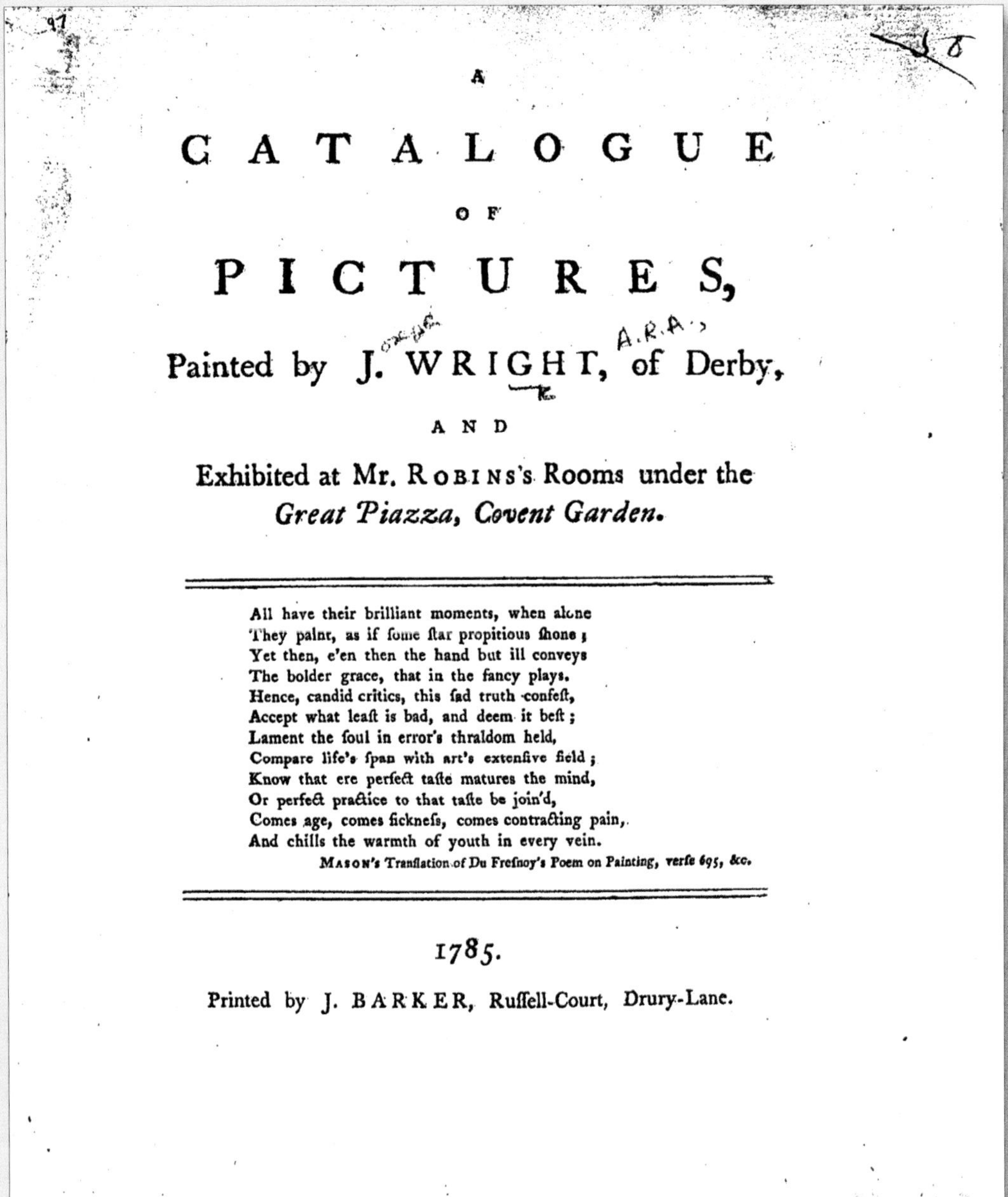

A

CATALOGUE

OF

PICTURES,

Painted by J. WRIGHT, of Derby,

AND

Exhibited at Mr. ROBINS's Rooms under the *Great Piazza, Covent Garden.*

All have their brilliant moments, when alone
They paint, as if some star propitious shone;
Yet then, e'en then the hand but ill conveys
The bolder grace, that in the fancy plays.
Hence, candid critics, this sad truth confest,
Accept what least is bad, and deem it best;
Lament the soul in error's thraldom held,
Compare life's span with art's extensive field;
Know that ere perfect taste matures the mind,
Or perfect practice to that taste be join'd,
Comes age, comes sickness, comes contracting pain,
And chills the warmth of youth in every vein.

MASON's Translation of Du Fresnoy's Poem on Painting, verse 695, &c.

1785.

Printed by J. BARKER, Russell-Court, Drury-Lane.

Fig. 1. Cover page of *A Catalogue of Pictures, Painted by J. Wright, of Derby, and Exhibited at Mr. Robins's Rooms under the Great Piazza, Covent Garden* (London: J. Barker, 1785) conceived alternative means of placing their work before the public. Wright was but one of a number of prominent personalities, including Copley and Thomas Gainsborough (1727–1788), opting to display works separately, and often as not highlighting pictures patriotic in theme.[22]

Included among the twenty-five pictures on show at Robins's Rooms were views of the continental and national landscape, alongside paintings on subjects suggested by or advised on by Hayley, such as *The Lady in Milton's Comus* and its companion *The Widow of an Indian Chief, watching the Arms of her Dead Husband*.[23] Hayley provided the verse and captions for the show's catalogue, establishing a series of interrelated, criss-crossing narratives around themes of war and peace, sentiment and stoic suffering. Lines from William Mason's 1783 translation of Charles Alphonse Dufresnoy's *De arte graphica*, perhaps the most influential of academic exegeses on the doctrine of *ut pictura poesis*, announced the exhibition (fig. 1). While this inclusion is indicative of the mutually supportive roles painting and poetry had in the exhibition more generally, they also made the artist's association with Horatian ideals of rural retirement explicit.[24] The selected lines originated in a section of Dufresnoy's work describing the need for study, and (alluding to Wright's maladies) the cost of a life spent in seclusion, where "Comes age, comes sickness, comes contracting pain, / And chills the warmth of youth in every vein." This life of dedicated, sequestered meditation is further indicated by the catalogue's identification of the painter as being "of Derby," a sobriquet that served to associate Wright with those literary figures with which he was most closely connected by the mid-1780s, who were identified as "of Eartham" like Hayley or "of Lichfield," as with Anna Seward (1747–1809), who also published verse in praise of the artist.[25] That Wright was "of Derby" may therefore been seen as suggestive of an artist not "of London," but at a remove or remote from the political factionalism and manoeuvring of the city's art world.

From a commercial standpoint Wright's venture was evidently a failure, as the business news of the *Public Advertiser* hinted on drawing a comparison with a similarly ill-fated rival one-man exhibition launched by George Carter (1737–1794): "Carter, as he very justly deserves, and Wright of Derby, as he very justly does *not* deserve, except for his caprice and spleen, (for Wright is a very fine painter) both are losers of their experiments of separate exhibitions."[26] In that year's crowded exhibition calendar these artists not only faced competition from the Royalists but a number of highly theatrical and spectacular rivals. On the same page of the 30 April 1785 edition of the *Morning Post* as Wright's display was advertised were to be found notices puffing Carter's show at rooms on Pall Mall, along with a "beautiful Moving Picture from The Eidophusikon," showing at the Exeter Change in the Strand with Thomas Jervais's productions in stained glass and "several capital Transparent Paintings, by Mr. De Loutherbourg, and Transparent Drawings by Mr P. Sandby." Wright's exhibition was most likely lost amid all of these competing claims on the attention of the city's audiences. Wright's failure to sell *A View of Gibraltar* or to produce a painting that might be readily translated into a print, so emulating a model of practice pursued so successfully by Copley, meant that there was to be no income beyond the evidently meagre takings on the door.

From a critical perspective, however, even taking in to account the significant number of notices clearly penned or sponsored by the painter's supporters, Wright's exhibition was a triumph, attracting extended and positive commentary, with the centrepiece drawing the most praise, one critic finding "his design is sublime, and his colouring natural and brilliant beyond description."[27] Another reviewer, finding it difficult to characterise fully the experience of *A View of Gibraltar*, argued: "It is impossible to speak in adequate terms of the several beauties of this picture: whether viewed near, or at some distance, it will equally please the eye of the rude and of the critical spectator. The painter has here arrived to the summit of his art, so that we may truly say of this collection, *Fins coronat opus*."[28] Such warm commendations differed markedly from the reception accorded to the Academy show, which opened a week later and only a few hundred yards from Wright's display. For the critic of the *General Advertiser*, in a far from uncommon verdict, that year's ensemble "disgraced the walls of the Academy." Accounting for this lamentable state of affairs the author gestured "to open affronts given to men of genius – to the total absence of Gainsborough, of Wright, and of Romney, who are disgusted with the government in the Academy."[29] "We are sorry that we cannot compliment the artists on their improvement of the English school," echoed the reviewer of the *London Chronicle*, who on surveying the walls found the eye "wearied with looking on a multitude of cold portraits."[30]

Wright's Covent Garden exhibition had been deliberately timed to coincide with and rival that of the Royalists, and much of the critical commentary around both shows understood the artist's actions in those terms.[31] A series of lengthy letters published in the *Public Advertiser*, signed by one "Timothy Tickle," addressed the Academy's treatment of "several artists of the first rank" who had abandoned Somerset House "on account, as it is said, of ill treatment they received from the leading members."[32] In a lengthy account of Wright's dealings with the Academy, Tickle argued that the artist "had been driven to make an exhibition of his own."[33] In this way, he presented Wright's show as an exemplary rallying point; suggestive of the ways in which the general decline in British art he and many other critics detected might be reversed. Wright's dedication to his art distinguished him from the monetary concerns of the majority who exhibited a few hundred yards away at Somerset House. This was an argument first ventured by Wright's collaborator and chief publicist in his *Ode* to the painter, and rehearsed once more in lines Hayley published in a London daily addressing the achievement of *A View of Gibraltar* on its public showing:

> Ye Sons of Albion view, with proud delight,
> This Rock that blazes in the tints of Wright;
> Behold the proof, that British minds and hearts,
> Are Honour's darlings, both in arms and arts:
> With double triumph here, let Britons say –
> Britons alone could rule this fiery fray:
> This miracle of art a Briton wrought,
> Painting as boldly as his Country fought.[34]

Thanks are due to Matthew Craske and Stephen Daniels for discussing aspects of this material with me.

1. Wright to William Hayley, 13 January 1783, Derby Local Studies Centre; see Barker 2009, Letter 46.
2. Nicolson 1968, no. 190; Derby Museum and Art Gallery.
3. "Royal Academy, 1778," the *Morning Chronicle, and London Advertiser*, 1 May 1778, p. 2. For a fuller account of Wright's showing at the Royal Academy this year and his relationship with that institution more generally, see John Bonehill, "'The eye of delicacy': Joseph Wright of Derby reviewed," in John Barrell, Mark Hallett and Sarah Monks, eds., *Living with the Royal Academy: Artistic Ideals and Experiences in Britain, 1768–1848* (forthcoming).
4. William Hayley, *An Epistle to an Eminent Painter* (London, 1778), p. 32.
5. Wright to William Hayley, 31 August 1783, Hayley MS 231-1949, Fitzwilliam Museum, Cambridge; see Barker 2009, Letter 50.
6. A selection of this correspondence has been published recently in Barker 2009, pp. 69–156.
7. Among the ten books inscribed with Wright's signature sold by Pickering and Chatto in 1991 were three titles by Hayley, and several others dedicated to or sponsored by the poet.
8. For a full account of Garvey's election and discussion of an offer of full Academician status made to Wright later, see William T. Whitley, *Artists and Their Friends in England, 1700–1799* (London: The Medici Society, 1928), vol. 1, pp. 340–341.
9. Anthony Pasquin [John Williams], *The Royal Academicians, A Farce* (London, 1786), p. 42.
10. William Hayley, *Memoirs of the Life and Writings of William Hayley, Esq.,* ed. John Johnson (London: Henry Colburn, 1823), vol. 1, p. 303.
11. William Hayley, *Ode to Mr. Wright of Derby* (Chichester: Dennett Jaques, 1783), p. 9.
12. Ibid., p. 10.
13. Wright to William Hayley, 3 December 1783, Derby Museum and Art Gallery; see Barker 2009, Letter 53.
14. The *Morning Chronicle, and London Advertiser*, 30 May 1783, p. 3.
15. The *London Gazette Extraordinary*, 8 November 1782, p. 3.
16. Horace Walpole, *Correspondence*, ed. W. S. Lewis (New Haven and London: Yale University Press, 1937–1983), vol. 35, p. 367.
17. Vicesimus Knox, *Essays, Moral and Literary* (London, 1778), p. 7. Knox's work exerted a considerable influence over Hayley, being quoted at length in the poet's *Epistle to an Eminent Painter.*
18. On these aspects of Copley's practice, see John Bonehill, "Exhibiting war: John Singleton Copley's *Siege of Gibraltar* and the staging of history," in John Bonehill and Geoff Quilley, eds., *Conflicting Visions: War and Visual Culture in Britain and France, c.1700–1830* (Aldershot: Ashgate, 2005), pp. 139–168. Wright's remarks on these issues come in the letter to Hayley dated 13 January 1783 (see note 1).
19. Wright to William Hayley, 9 March 1783, Hayley MS 231-1949, Fitzwilliam Museum, Cambridge (not in Barker 2009).
20. Wright to William Hayley, 17 February 1785, pasted in an extra-illustrated copy of William Bemrose, *The Life and Works of Joseph Wright, Commonly Called "Wright of Derby"* (Derby: Bemrose and Sons, 1885), now in Derby Museum and Art Gallery; see also Barker 2009, Letter 63. Hayley 1785 also clearly states that the painter was intent on producing a second picture.
21. The *General Evening Post*, 6 January 1785, p. 4. Wright instructed Hayley to place this notice in the press: see Wright to William Hayley, 22 December 1784, Derby Local Studies Centre (Barker 2009, Letter 61).
22. Although the causes of these artists' differences with the Academy varied, it appears likely that there was at least a shared concern to exert greater control over the conditions in which their works were to be seen. Contemporary accounts of Gainsborough's relationship with the Academy indicate his unhappiness with the "improper situation" of his pictures in the Great Room at Somerset House, leading him to exhibit his paintings in his own studio (see the *Public Advertiser*, 26 May 1785, p. 2).
23. *The Lady in Milton's Comus* (Nicolson 1968, no. 234; Walker Art Centre, Liverpool), *The Widow of an Indian Chief, watching the Arms of her Dead Husband* (Nicolson 1968, no. 243; Derby Museum and Art Gallery). This section condenses material first discussed in Bonehill 2008.
24. This is an aspect of Wright's artistic persona discussed more fully in Bonehill, "'The eye of delicacy'" (see note 3).
25. Anna Seward, "Verses addressed to Mr. WRIGHT of Derby. By Miss SEWARD. On his having PAINTED HER FATHER'S PICTURE," *The Gentleman's Magazine* (August 1783), p. 693.
26. The *Public Advertiser*, 1 June 1785, p. 3.
27. The *General Evening Post*, 14–16 April 1785, p. 4.
28. The *Morning Post, and Daily Advertiser*, 20 April 1785, p. 2.
29. The *General Advertiser*, 2 May 1785, p. 3.
30. The *London Chronicle*, 26 April 1785, p. 5.
31. Writing to Hayley two months prior to the opening of the exhibition, Wright expressed the need "to get the start of the Royalists" (17 February 1785, pasted in an extra-illustrated copy of Bemrose, *Joseph Wright*, [see note 20]; see also Barker 2009, Letter 63). Wright's exhibition opened on Monday, 11 April 1785.
32. The *Public Advertiser*, 17 May 1785, p. 1.
33. Ibid., p. 2. Letters published by Tickle in the 23 May and 26 May 1785 editions of the *Public Advertiser* focused on the circumstances surrounding George Stubbs's and Thomas Gainsborough's disputes with the Royal Academy.
34. The *Morning Post, and Daily Advertiser*, 7 May 1785, p. 3. On Hayley's own antipathy towards the Academy at this moment, see Joseph Farington, *The Diary of Joseph Farington*, ed. Kenneth Garlick and Angus Macintyre (New Haven and London: Yale University Press, 2002), vol. 3, p. 678.

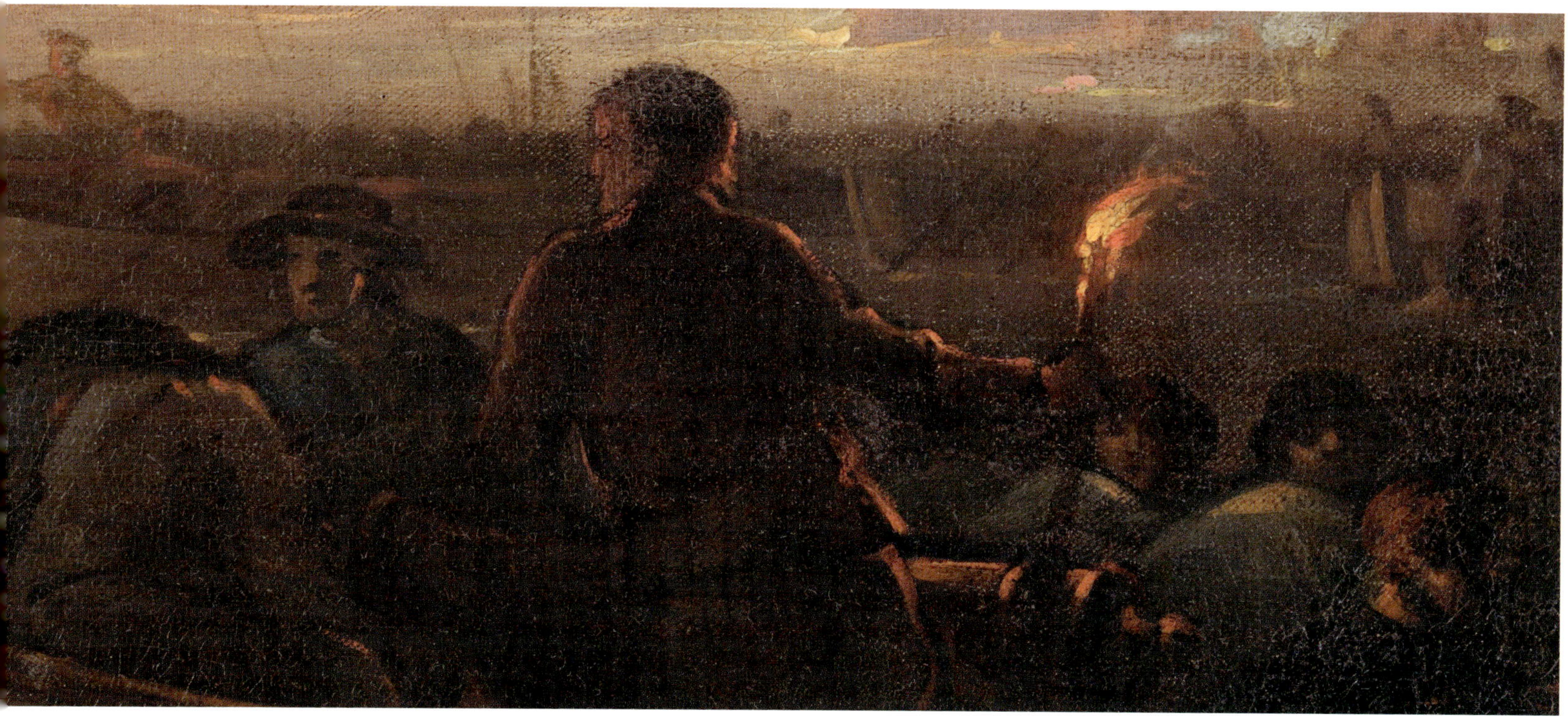

QUEST FOR FIRE:
RETRIEVING JOSEPH WRIGHT OF DERBY'S *VIEW OF GIBRALTAR*

DAVID DE WITT

THE SUCCESSFUL DEFENCE of the Rock of Gibraltar against a massive seaborne artillery attack on the night of 13 September 1782 sparked a rush among British painters to depict their nation's dramatic victory. Among their number was Joseph Wright of Derby, who expressed his interest in a letter to his friend William Hayley of 9 January 1783, citing the encouragement of friends.[1] The night battle, already compelling in its appeal to nationalist sentiment, offered Wright a stage for his famous mastery of firelight. He had by then built up a considerable repertoire of scenes featuring effects of light; nonetheless, this military theme represented a leap, and his correspondence betrays some trepidation. Wright presented his painting to the public as the centrepiece of a remarkable one-man show in London on 11 April 1785. Despite fetching a high price, *A View of Gibraltar during the destruction of the Spanish Floating Batteries, on the 13th of September, 1782* later fell into obscurity. In his 1968 catalogue raisonné on the artist, Benedict Nicolson declared it lost.

In 1967, a painting of this subject surfaced in Milwaukee. It was covered with a great deal of overpaint, which was removed to reveal that the work had been badly over-cleaned, especially in the area of the smoke clouds that fill the upper half. The comparison to Wright's work was further complicated by the unconventional theme for him, but Nicolson did subsequently accept it as the long-missing work.[2] Twenty years later it was again studied, by Judy Egerton, researching Wright's works for a monographic exhibition in 1990. She rejected the attribution, although her criteria are not entirely compelling, and she appeared unaware of its condition. Nicolson did see it cleaned, but it was soon thereafter covered up by overpaint meant to salvage its appearance. This obstacle likewise applies to Elizabeth Barker's more recent comment on the painting's "soft" handling.[3]

The Agnes Etherington Art Centre acquired the work in 2001 with the aim of investigating Wright's authorship. It was technically analysed using a variety of methods by conservation scientist Kate Helwig and her colleagues at the Canadian Centre for Conservation in Ottawa, and thoroughly cleaned of varnish and overpaint by professor Barbara Klempan at Queen's University. The resulting evidence of the execution and materials proved consistent with Wright's practice, especially his distinctive use of dead-colouring, as Klempan indicates in her essay for this publication. The absence of underdrawing similarly concurs with previous infrared reflectography research on his paintings.[4] With the condition and the surviving pictorial evidence made available and legible, it is now more feasible and meaningful to examine and judge this painting with respect to the question of the attribution. Only the boats and figures to the right and the ships in the centre of the canvas bear scrutiny as finished work by Wright; the rest of *A View of Gibraltar* must be judged solely in terms of its composition, as it has been cleaned down to the underlying preparatory layers. This essay's systematic review of the painting's available stylistic evidence reveals a wide range of links to Wright's development leading up to and including the period when he executed *A View of Gibraltar*, lending support to Nicolson's attribution.

This painting depicts a stunning British military victory that came in the wake of the humbling loss of the American colonies. The Spanish and the French had been blockading the stronghold at Gibraltar since 1779, and in 1782 they planned a decisive attack using special floating artillery batteries designed to sustain defensive fire. The barrage started around ten o'clock on 12 September.[5] Because the British were able to fire far more red-hot shot than expected, and with considerable accuracy, the batteries succumbed spectacularly. By three o'clock the following morning most of them were burning. When the British moved in on them in gunboats, they saw that many of their crew were still aboard, left to their fate. They immediately undertook to rescue them, only retreating when the batteries' powder magazines began exploding, around five o'clock. This particular action, demonstrating humanity in the face of danger, attracted a number of artists, such as Conrad Martin Metz,[6] John Cleveley,[7] James Jefferys,[8] and John Keyse Sherwin (fig. 2). The rescue was led by Captain Roger Curtis, whom Wright later singled out as a source of information, which he anxiously sought in order to avoid errors in a genre unfamiliar to him. This choice could have signalled an interest in emphasizing the rescue action. We know it was manifest in his painting, from Wright's own description, and those of William Hayley and others.[9] More speculatively, this scene may have resonated with the humanitarian inclination of an artist who followed Rousseau, and befriended abolitionists such as Erasmus Darwin.[10]

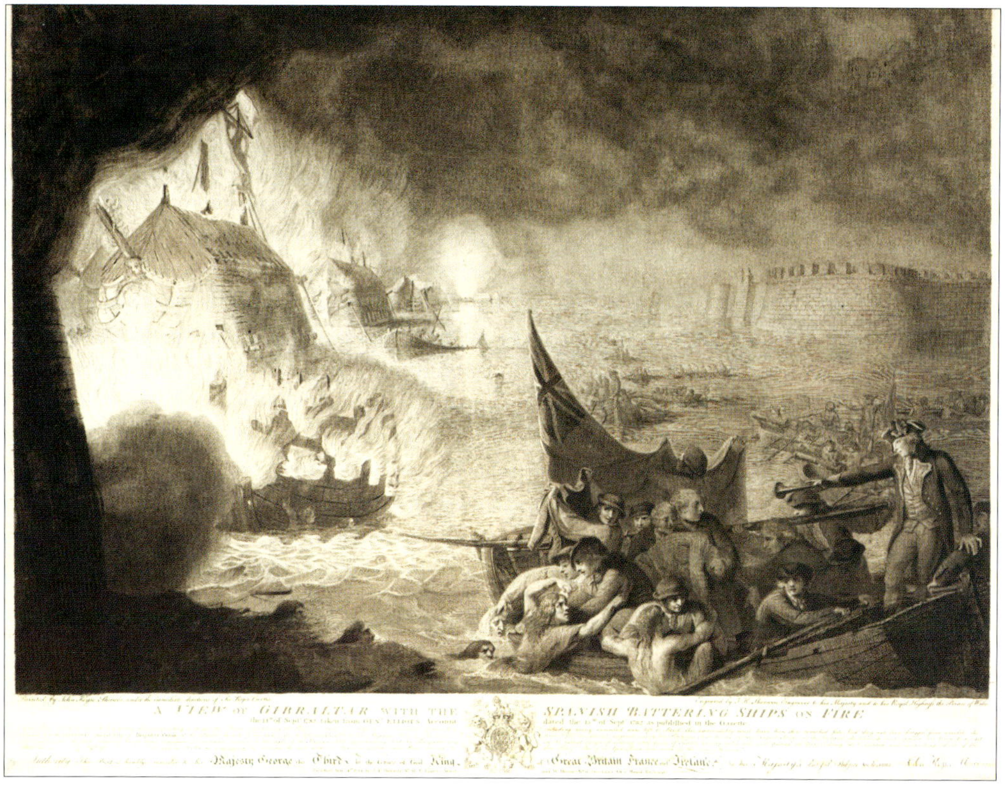

Fig. 2.
John Keyse Sherwin
A View of Gibraltar with the Spanish Battering Ships on Fire
1784, etching and engraving
46.2 × 60.6 cm

In Wright's *View of Gibraltar*, Captain Curtis stands in the middle of a gunboat at the lower right corner of the canvas, while at the prow a man pulls a sailor out of the water. In the distance rise the British fortifications of Gibraltar, a high seashore wall with cannon ports. The outlines of a bastion and cannon smoke frame Curtis's figure with an artifice typical for Wright. The Captain engages his entire body in the gesture of command, his right arm eloquently pointing with his sword toward the action to the left, his other arm sweeping up high to underscore the urgency of the situation, while his bold open stance signals his authority.

Across from him to the left is a floating battery, with its distinctive peaked roof and oversized cannon ports, in full blaze. A large expanse of cloth falls over the left side. This is the separate cover that was constantly wetted with water supplied by pumps below, to suppress fires. The painting poignantly underlines the pumps' failure as a key element of the dilemma befalling the Spanish sailors, revealing a technical interest consonant with pictures such as Wright's *A Philosopher giving that lecture on the Orrery, in which a Lamp is put in place of the Sun*[11] and *An Experiment on a Bird in the Air Pump* (fig. 3).[12] The Spaniards are now pathetic figures scattered about the left half of the composition, their heads emerging from the water as they swim away from the batteries, with others still perched on top of the bowsprit of the doomed vessel at the far left. In contrast, Curtis's bold figure forms a strong diagonal line leaning left, answered by the forms of smoke clouds above swept by the wind in the other direction. The clouds fill the entire upper half of the composition, their monumental forms rising from, and thus amplifying, the action below.

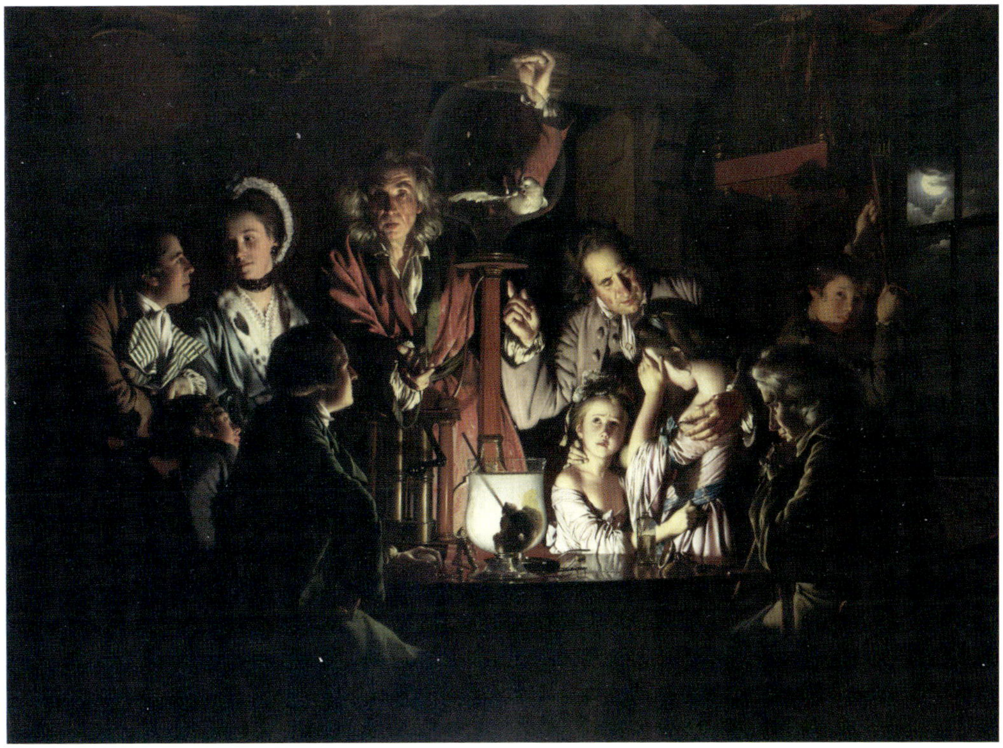

Fig. 3.
Joseph Wright of Derby
An Experiment on a Bird in the Air Pump
1768, oil on canvas, 183 × 244 cm
London, National Gallery (NG725)

Wright clearly pursued effect rather than specific narrative clarity. The figures are small and often dark, while the burning batteries dominate the composition, in particular the one near centre, with its many flashes of fire through gun ports and elsewhere, and sweeping flames towering above. Another battery appears immediately beside it to the left, farther back and turned more to the right. Strikingly juxtaposed to these, a third battery farther away and to the left is still in action, issuing whitish round puffs of cannon smoke quite distinct from the blackish plumes above. At the left edge emerges the fourth battery, in flames, with sailors trying to escape. The deliberate variation in the ships and figures distinguishes this composition from other depictions of the theme. John Keyse Sherwin's for example emphasizes rows of ships and clusters of figures, to generate a more imposing effect. The variation here characterizes Wright's pictorial approach, used to enliven landscapes and historical scenes.

The boats in the foreground are largely cast in darkness, which serves to isolate and accentuate Curtis and a second officer to the right, who are lit by the blazes. Equally significant is the separate area of local illumination to Curtis's left where the light of a torch grazes the contours of the nearby figures, in particular the one with his back to us. Such edge lighting appears in several other fire pictures by Wright, in particular his slightly later *Cottage on Fire* in Derby.[13] Indeed, virtuoso displays of lighting appear throughout *A View of Gibraltar*: at the left edge where the fleeing sailors and the bowsprit structure catch the light emerging from within the burning vessel, and in the carefully articulated firelight coming through the ports of the failing battery at centre. These parts of the canvas point directly to Wright, and to his motivation for taking on this contemporary historical theme.

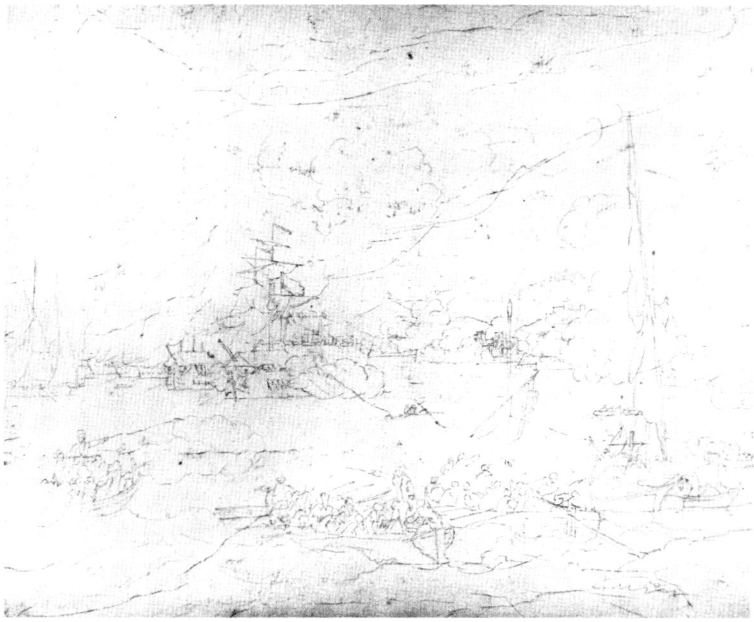

Fig. 4.
Joseph Wright of Derby
A Sea Battle (The Destruction of the Spanish Floating Batteries)
pencil, 29.2 × 33.3 cm
Derby, Derby Museum and Art Gallery (207)

The provenance of Wright's painting is described elsewhere in this publication. By the time *A View of Gibraltar* was offered for sale in the United States in 1923, it was dubiously attributed to John Singleton Copley, with a cynical eye to the local market.[14] Biruta Erdmann first returned the attribution to Wright in a 1973 article,[15] indicating its close relationship to a drawing in Derby, *A Sea Battle (The Destruction of the Spanish Floating Batteries)* (fig. 4).[16] This sheet, drawn in the wiry contours characteristic of Wright's landscape drawings, shows a slightly earlier moment in the battle, as gunboats approach the batteries from a distance. Captain Curtis commands the action with a sword in his outstretched hand, as in *A View of Gibraltar*. In the drawing the scale is smaller and the view wider, but the main components reflect the painting: Curtis and his boat are positioned to the right, with the Rock behind them, and the nearest batteries to the left. In an article published posthumously, Benedict Nicolson added his support to Erdmann's attribution to Wright, which he based partly on the figures, and partly on the strength of the composition.[17]

A View of Gibraltar is a primarily pictorial arrangement, showing a sophisticated distribution and balance of points of interest in a measured rhythm. This aesthetic approach stands in contrast to the later interpretation of the siege by the prominent history painter John Singleton Copley (1738–1815), in the collection of the Guildhall Art Gallery in London.[18] Copley shows a mounted General Elliot on the garrison wall, surrounded by his men, in imposingly large scale in the foreground, across from floating batteries that loom unrealistically close, compressing the space. It is more of a group portrait of the battle's heroes, with the action as a staged backdrop, than the threatening drama of the darker scene in *A View of Gibraltar*, which accords with the comment of a visitor to Wright's exhibition, claiming never to have seen "shadows painted so little like substance as those in the foreground."[19] Its overpowering effect of light, as well as the substantial forms of the composition, distinguishes it from battle scenes produced by naval specialists,[20] such as one of 1782 by Thomas Whitcombe (around 1752–around 1824), with its small-scale ships and distant landscape.[21]

The Kingston canvas, with its focus on Captain Curtis leading the rescue, bears striking comparison to the print by John Keyse Sherwin (fig. 2) in a number of aspects: the position of Captain Curtis's boat at lower right, his pose, the nearby floating battery in flames, and another at the left edge. Wright's composition is at the same time more expansive and complex, his figures in turn more poised and elegant. Sherwin asserts in his inscription that his original painting (now lost) was made "under the immediate direction of Sir Roger Curtis." In the end, Wright failed to make this contact.[22] Sherwin's print appeared in September 1784, too late to affect Wright's composition, which must have been well established by then. Wright likely had to draw on verbal accounts detailing the location of the various vessels and combatants.

While *A View of Gibraltar* contrasts with depictions of the battle by other artists, it takes a place in a line of pictures in Wright's oeuvre that feature effects of artificial light. After studying in London with Thomas Hudson (1701–1779) in the 1750s, Wright was established as a portraitist in his native Derby. In the 1760s he embarked on his celebrated "subject pictures" such as *The Orrery*, an interior scene with candlelight. He further established himself as a master of candlelight effects with works such as *Three Persons Viewing the Gladiator by Candlelight*,[23] and his famous scientific tableau, *The Air Pump*. The latter work shows a demonstration of the effects of a vacuum pump on a bird in an enclosed chamber, and is often cited with respect to intellectual and technological developments in Derbyshire. Wright dramatized this scene with a range of emotional reactions in a varied group of onlookers, including distraught girls and a distracted pair of lovers. A single lamp on the table casts its light upwards, producing a variety of striking chiaroscuro effects that heighten the tension of the scene considerably. As Nicolson posited, Wright took many cues from Dutch Caravaggist paintings of the seventeenth century,[24] and likely also knew the later candlelight scenes by Godfried Schalcken (1643–1703), who was in London between 1692 and 1697. Schalcken's smooth execution certainly comes closer to Wright than do the Caravaggisti.[25]

In the 1770s, Wright expanded into "firelight pictures," with stronger light sources and wider views, depicting smithies and iron forges. His reputation in this specialty spread, as testified in the reported response of fellow painter Richard Wilson to Wright's proposal to exchange pictures: "With all my heart, Wright, I'll give you air, and you'll give me fire."[26] One of these, *An Iron Forge viewed from Without* of 1773 in the Hermitage[27] shows Wright's compositional strategy for sustaining the effect of light throughout the painting: the area near the centre features strong light, accentuated by contrasting dark forms, especially the smith bending over to hold the iron. Lesser areas of light appear farther away from the centre, in evenly spaced, discrete episodes, emerging from and isolated by the surrounding darkness. These maintain clarity even in the obscurity of darkness, conjuring a slightly surreal air.

Wright travelled to Italy in 1774–1775, and worked briefly in Bath before returning to Derby permanently, enjoying great success and befriending intellectual luminaries such as Erasmus Darwin (1731–1802). He expanded into landscape and literary themes, even contributing to Josiah Boydell's Shakespeare Gallery. His *View of Gibraltar*, however, would be his only foray into contemporary history. Wright often pursued firelight effects in his landscape paintings. He regularly depicted Vesuvius in eruption, and one of the most spectacular of these paintings, *An Eruption of Mount Vesuvius, with the Procession of St Januarius' Head* of 1778 (fig. 5),[28] exploits the flash of the blast as well as its reflections in the smoke clouds rising

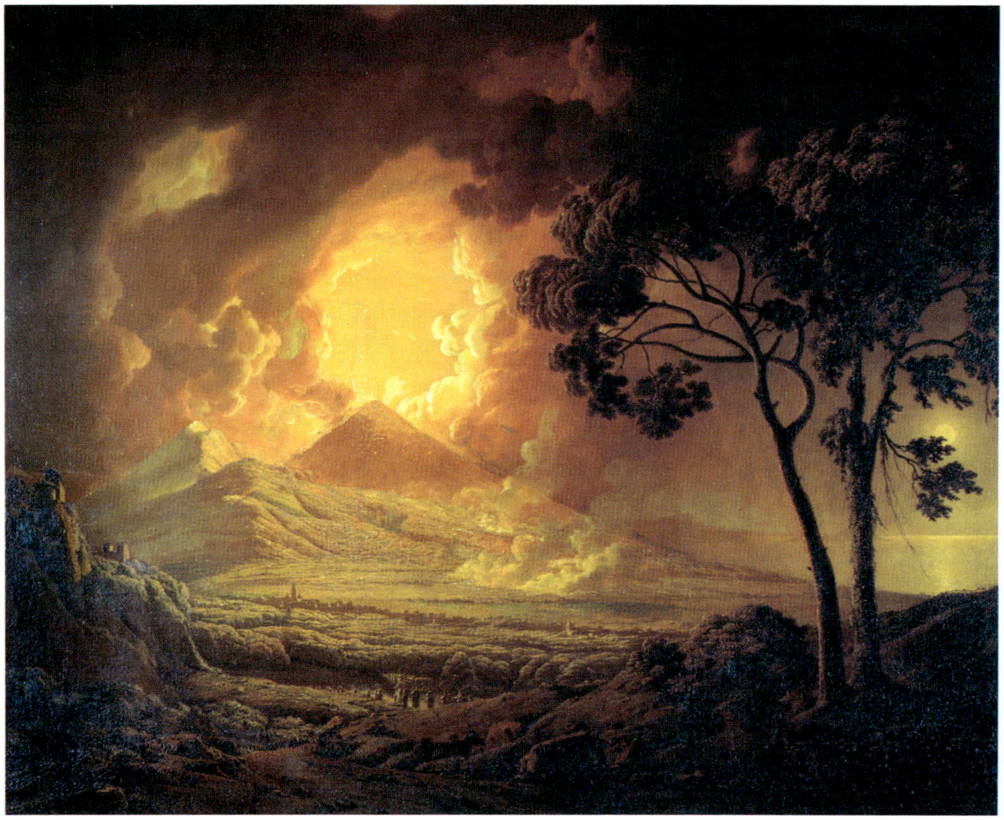

Fig. 5.
Joseph Wright of Derby
An Eruption of Mount Vesuvius, with the Procession of St Januarius' Head
1778, oil on canvas, 162 × 213.4 cm
Moscow, Pushkin State Museum of Fine Arts

above, in the hilly landscape, and in trees to the right. Wright structured his composition with a sophisticated asymmetry, the volcano to the left balanced by a second, isolated focus farther off to the right: the full moon and its reflection in the Bay of Naples below. The pictorial space is further articulated with other smaller and varied episodes: a shaded rock in the foreground, illuminated cliffs to the left, and the procession in the middle distance.

Of Wright's paintings, *An Eruption of Mount Vesuvius* compares most closely in compositional strategies to *A View of Gibraltar*. Wright's painting of the siege shows a similar asymmetrical arrangement, with the burning battery to the left, across from the lesser light consisting of the figure of Captain Curtis standing to the right. As with *An Eruption of Mount Vesuvius*, there are several discrete areas of focus: the lighted figures on the bowsprit at left; the distant floating battery shrouded in whitish smoke; a boat of fleeing sailors in the murky waters in front of it; the bastion at left with smoke puffs above it; the torchlit area to the right of Curtis and a cluster of figures behind him in the same boat, including another captain, perhaps Elliot. The effect of light at centre is accentuated through sharp contrasts at the gun ports and the reflections in the sky and the fortifications, an approach already seen in *An Iron Forge*. It is clearly the same pictorial intelligence at work in all of these works: patient, orderly, clear and occasionally naïve in spirit.

Even with the loss of paint and glazing layers to over-cleaning, what remains of the handling of the sky in *A View of Gibraltar* offers critical points of comparison to *An Eruption of Mount Vesuvius*. The loose and open red and yellow brush strokes outlining the reflections at the edges of smoke clouds above

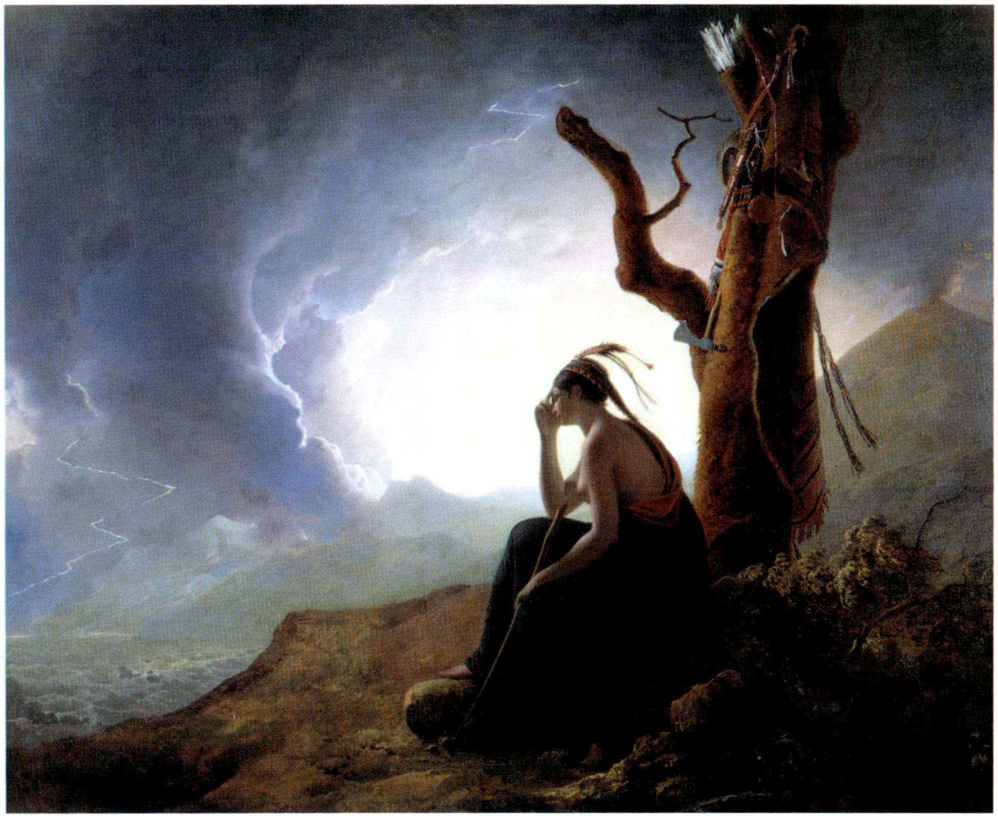

Fig. 6.
Joseph Wright of Derby
The Widow of an Indian Chief, watching the Arms of her Dead Husband
1785, oil on canvas, 101.6 × 127 cm
Derby, Derby Museum and Art Gallery
(1961-508/6)

the blazing battery are similar to those above the volcano. Also, as with the *An Eruption of Mount Vesuvius*, there are softly brushed areas of red that suggest a glowing reflection in the rising body of the smoke. Less subtly, the sweeping diagonal mass of smoke clouds amplifies the violence of the fire in both works. It appears that Wright's earlier depiction of Vesuvius provided solutions for staging a great spectacle of light in a wide landscape, for the fiery battle scene. *An Eruption of Mount Vesuvius* further demonstrates that Wright could resort to loose and free brush strokes, one of the most unconventional aspects of *A View of Gibraltar*.

The dramatic sky in *A View of Gibraltar* also resonates closely with one of the other paintings hanging in Wright's 1785 exhibition in Robins's Rooms: *The Widow of an Indian Chief, watching the Arms of her Dead Husband*, now in the Derby Museum (fig. 6).[29] The opening in the clouds above the widow closely echoes the smoke plumes bursting from both sides of the burning ship in the siege painting, even following the same diagonal sweep. Their monumental forms likewise expand from a smaller form below: the burning ship or the figure of the widow, respectively. Wright set the head and shoulders of the widow directly against a burst of light over the horizon, using light contrast to highlight his main focus, much as with the main floating battery in *A View of Gibraltar*. Wright's tendency to arrange discrete and isolated passages with their own space, evident throughout his painting of the siege, resurfaces in *The Widow of an Indian Chief* in the volcano to the right of the tree, the branch, and the lightning flash to the left. Both works show his conspicuous pursuit of variation in motifs.

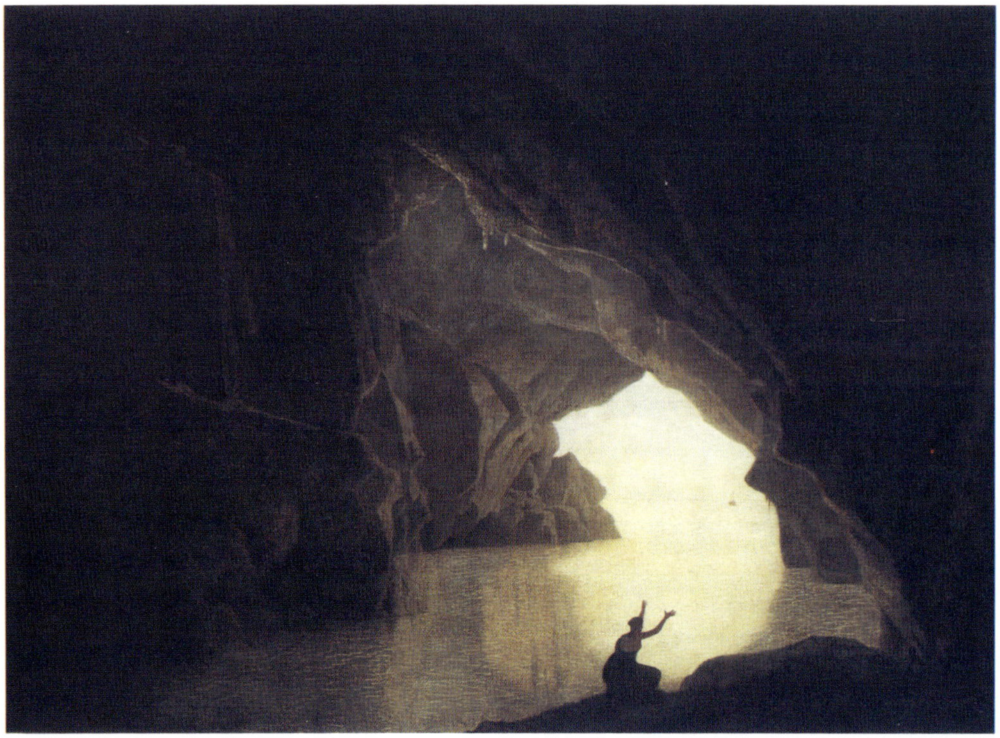

Fig. 7.
Joseph Wright of Derby
A Grotto in the Gulf of Salernum, with the figure of Julia, banished from Rome
1780, oil on canvas, 114.3 × 175.3 cm
Private collection

Wright's use of colour in these canvases is also telling. Pink and pale yellow hues appear in the areas of illumination in both works, an imaginative combination. Benedict Nicolson lamented Wright's development of fanciful artifice ("the dream") in the late 1780s and beyond, away from his earlier frank naturalism.[30] It is, however, consistent with his pursuit of effect, which takes on qualities of the sublime, and distances him from his fellow history painters such as Copley and West.[31]

The figure style in *A View of Gibraltar* raises one final point of comparison with other works from his oeuvre. Captain Curtis's slender proportions, sinuous curved lines and abstracted forms, and the aquiline profile of the officer to his right both accord with Wright's interest in classicism starting in the late 1770s, exemplified by such works as *The Corinthian Maid*,[32] painted for Josiah Wedgwood. His new figural aesthetic emphasizes elegance, incorporating tapered shapes, especially of the arms, often with expressively pointing or spread fingers that deliver a frisson of dramatic tension. The small, dynamic and accentuated figure of the abandoned Julia, daughter of Augustus, in *A Grotto in the Gulf of Salernum, with the figure of Julia, banished from Rome* of 1780 (fig. 7),[33] supplies a direct precedent for that of Captain Curtis in *A View of Gibraltar*, who is in turn echoed in the figure of Antigonus in Wright's Shakespearian scene, *Antigonus in the Storm* (1792).[34] Curtis's expressively sweeping pose likewise echoes Wright's larger scale figure of Juliet in *Romeo and Juliet* (1790), another Shakespearian painting.[35]

The abovementioned aspects of *A View of Gibraltar*: composition, light, colour and figure style, generally did not figure into the comments of Judy Egerton. Her surprising complaint about the "lumpishness" of the figures is gainsaid by Captain Curtis's silhouette, and its relationship to figures such as that of Augustus's daughter. Her claim that the painting fails to "extract maximum light and shade effects from the burning ships" overlooks the orchestration of light contrast at its central focus.[36] The only previous scholar to see the painting fully cleaned was Benedict Nicolson. His judgement was, by contrast, positive.[37] The recent study by Barbara Klempan concludes that, soon after Nicolson's viewing, the painting was covered up again with overpaint, likely to save time and salvage the appearance of a badly damaged painting. The failure of subsequent scholars, including Egerton, to consider overpaint and condition seriously undermines their assessments.

The impact of Wright's sustained difficulties in completing *A View of Gibraltar* must also be considered. In his letters, the artist complained that he was unable to obtain the first-hand report he sought from Captain Curtis, and that he was laid up for nearly an entire year before he could resume work on the painting. He then put himself under considerable time pressure by committing to an exhibition in 1785, for which he had to complete a number of important paintings. He was again sidelined for another two months, late in 1784.[38] The finishing touches on *A View of Gibraltar* were announced in mid-February, less than two months before the exhibition opening, and by then Wright was deeply concerned about the reception of the work. It is in this light that we must read his comments to William Hayley on the painting:

> After all I fear it is not the picture you expect to see, as the action is not principal & at too great a distance to discriminate particulars; even the men in the Gunboats that lie just off the New Mole (w.[ch] makes a fine dark foreground to the picture) are not more than an inch high, however the floating Batteries in different degrees of burning make a fine blaze, & illuminate in a striking manner the noble Rock of Gib.[39]

Wright then urges Hayley, in writing the exhibition's catalogue, to emphasize that a second painting was planned that would feature more of the action; an intention he had already declared early in 1783.[40] Yet Wright's anxiety and defensive tone are reason enough to suspect some exaggeration in characterizing his painting as a sweeping view with small-scale ships and figures. Many of the competing depictions, of which John Keyse Sherwin's is an example, employed large-scale figures, and Wright was likely contrasting his approach to theirs. The gunboat crews in *A View of Gibraltar* are indeed small, although larger than the inch Wright cites, which Elizabeth Barker seizes as a reason to dismiss an attribution to Wright of this painting.[41] Wright must have used this measure as a general fixed expression, as such small figures would not have stood out on a canvas of some sixty inches high, let alone legibly present any of the human action, which Wright nonetheless claimed to have depicted.

Wright's haste could also explain the loose brushwork that appears in several places, most notably at the right edge, where one of leaning figures in the gunboat consists of a few open strokes. The unfurled sail at the left edge also appears to have been left without a finishing layer, and in the sky above it, a dark cloud is conjured with an open swirl of looping brush strokes. These areas, though assured, are unconventional for Wright, but even more so for any of his contemporaries. Far more likely, they point to an artist under time pressure to depict this theme, and to have struggled with it as a type outside of his usual range: Joseph Wright of Derby. It is possible that some of the sketchy passages also reveal Wright's preparatory layers of dead colour.

After *A View of Gibraltar*'s recent cleaning and cautious inpainting, we are now confronted with a great deal of the original depiction of the battle scene, providing much more accurate visual and technical information on which to base an assessment. It has lost all of the glazing that Wright used to achieve subtle modeling and crisp edges, especially in softer substances such as clouds. The surviving opaque strokes and red reflections compare closely with the earlier *An Eruption of Mount Vesuvius*. Also legible is the careful orchestration of illumination, fully in line with the development of Wright's celebrated scenes of candle- and firelight, of which *An Eruption of Mount Vesuvius* supplies a tellingly close precedent. Equally important, what remains of *A View of Gibraltar* reveals Wright's characteristically cautious and methodical approach to composition, arranging multiple discrete and isolated elements, and varying his motifs. Homage to Wright's arrangement even appears in a later depiction of a naval conflagration, *The Battle of the Nile* (1800) by Philip James de Loutherbourg (1740–1812), which also shows a blazing ship to the left of centre, and a boat of rescuers at lower right. Typically, De Loutherbourg conceived of these areas as unified masses.[42] Wright's contemporaries tended to connect their motifs organically, forming larger entities to generate force and monumentality. Light, articulated with variation and stark contrasts, was Wright's chief means of creating powerful effect.

When we look past the condition of *A View of Gibraltar* and focus on the still-legible composition, light effects and figures, rich and telling similarities to Wright's other paintings emerge that lend credence to Benedict Nicolson's attribution. There are numerous affinities, even in figure style and colour use, with the imaginative scenes that Wright was painting at the same time and that were destined for the same exhibition in which it was to be the highlight, such as *The Widow of an Indian Chief*. The Kingston painting shows Wright's pictorial sensibility at work. In it, he achieved his famed effect of firelight, which was after all a motivation for taking up this challenging theme.

1. Wright to William Hayley, 13 January 1783. Derby: Derby Museum and Art Gallery; see Barker 2009, Letter 46.
2. Letter from Benedict Nicolson to Alfred Bader, 28 January 1972, Agnes Etherington Art Centre object file: "I think it probably is the Wright of Derby sold to Milnes … some of the groups of sailors and officers in the foreground are sufficiently well preserved to look like Wrights, and the general composition is impressive." The attribution was confirmed in Nicolson's article of addenda to Wright's oeuvre, published posthumously; see Nicolson 1988, p. 745.
3. See Barker 2009, p. 7 note 22.
4. Rica Jones, "Notes for conservators on Joseph Wright of Derby's technique and studio practice," *The Conservator* 15 (1991), pp. 13–27. Ian Hodkinson and Deborah Child identified a rare exception in Kingston: *Cut Through the Rock, Cromford*, also in this exhibition (cat. 5): Ian S. Hodkinson and Deborah M. Child, "An 18th-Century Artist-Applied Lining: Joseph Wright of Derby's *Cut Through the Rock at Cromford*," *Journal of the American Institute for Conservation* 34, no. 3 (1995), p. 38. Rica Jones cites Wright's systematic use of dead-colouring, instead of underdrawing, to plan his compositions. See Jones 1990, p. 267.
5. See John Drinkwater, *A History of the Late Siege of Gibraltar*. 2nd ed. (London: J. Johnson, T. and J. Egerton, and J. Edwards, 1786), pp. 284–289; and René Chartrand, *Gibraltar 1779–83: The Great Siege* (Oxford: Osprey, 2006), pp. 65–83.
6. Ambrose William Warren, after Conrad Martin Metz, *Sir Roger Curtis gallantly exerting himself in preserving the Spaniards at Gibraltar*, 1802, etching and engraving, 16.2 × 21.1 cm. The drawing for this print is in the British Museum: brush and grey wash over graphite, 15.3 × 9.7 cm (1863,0214.767). The print was published in George Courtney Lyttleton, *The history of England from the earliest dawn of authentic record to the ultimate ratification of the general peace at Amiens, 1802* (London: J. Stratford, 1803).
7. Charles Tomkins and Francis Jukes, after John Cleveley, *Defeat of the Floating Batteries before Gibraltar on the Night of the 13th. of Sept. 1782*, 1786, aquatint, 29.1 × 38.0 cm.
8. James Jefferys, *The Scene Before Gibraltar with the Destruction of the Spanish Floating Batteries*, around 1784, oil on canvas, 245 × 160 cm, Maidstone, Kent: Maidstone Museum and Bentlif Gallery (22.1891). My thanks to Clare Caless for this information.
9. Wright's description of his painting, in his letter to Hayley of 17 February 1785 (see note 22, below), including reference to the boats in the foreground. Hayley dwells on the rescue in his *Ode to Mr. Wright of Derby*, a preliminary announcement of, and puff for, the painting: "Ye shall not perish: no! ye hapless brave / Reckless of peril thro' the fiery wave / See! British mercy steers, each prostrate foe to save." The rescue action is also cited in a handwritten note by J. Galpine added to the entry in the copy of the 1806 sale catalogue at the Metropolitan Museum of Art, New York (see Provenance): "one more Glorious Action sav'd 350 lives"; see Getty Provenance Index Br-427, no. 60.

10. On the influence of Rousseau and Darwin on Wright, see Nicolson 1968, vol. 1, p. 5.
11. Joseph Wright of Derby, *A Philosopher giving that Lecture on the Orrery, in which a Lamp is put in place of the Sun*, 1766, oil on canvas, 147.3 × 203.2 cm, Derby: Derby Museum and Art Gallery (1884-168); see Nicolson 1968, vol. 1, p. 235, no. 190; Egerton 1990, pp. 54–55, no. 18.
12. See Nicolson 1968, vol. 1, p. 235, no. 192; Egerton 1990, pp. 58–59, no. 21.
13. Joseph Wright of Derby, *Cottage on Fire*, around 1790, oil on canvas, 63.5 × 76.2 cm, Derby: Derby Museum and Art Gallery (1936-637); see Nicolson 1968, vol. 1, pp. 92, 270, no. 303. On edge lighting in both works, see Erdmann 1974, p. 271 note 14.
14. Letter from N. L. Ehrich to Judge Nathaniel Sears, 7 August 1923; photocopy in object file, Agnes Etherington Art Centre.
15. See Erdmann 1974, pp. 270–272, fig. 49.
16. See Nicolson 1968, vol. 1, p. 120 note 2 (as dated around 1772).
17. See note 2.
18. John Singleton Copley, *The Defeat of the Floating Batteries at Gibraltar, September 1782*, 1783–1791, oil on canvas, 543 × 754 cm, London: Guildhall Art Gallery.
19. Edward Bradbury attributes this passage to "an authority of standing"; see Bradbury 1883, p. 595. Bemrose quotes "a notice of the Press"; see Bemrose 1885, p. 75.
20. John Bonehill makes a similar observation; see Bonehill 2008, p. 530. Hayley, in his catalogue to Wright's 1785 exhibition, also specifies that this picture combines the scenery with the action; see Hayley 1785, p. 8.
21. Thomas Whitcombe, *The Destruction of the Floating Batteries at Gibraltar, 13 September 1782*, oil on canvas, 76 × 122 cm, Greenwich: National Maritime Museum (BCH0451).
22. This is Nicolson's conclusion, based on a letter from Wright to Hayley of 17 February 1785, on completion of the painting, in which the artist still complains of ignorance of naval matters. London: National Portrait Gallery, in an extra-illustrated copy of Bemrose 1885 (Barker 2009, Letter 63); see Nicolson 1968, vol. 1, p. 160.
23. Joseph Wright of Derby, *Three Persons Viewing the Gladiator by Candlelight*, 1764/65, oil on canvas, 101.6 × 121.9 cm, United Kingdom: private collection. See Nicolson 1968, vol. 1, p. 234, no. 188; Egerton 1990, pp. 61–63, no. 22.
24. Nicolson 1968, vol. 1, pp. 47–50. David Solkin draws a connection between Wright's attention to Dutch art and his loyalty towards the Society of Artists of Great Britain, and more troubled relationship with the Royal Academy; see David H. Solkin, "Joseph Wright of Derby and the Sublime Art of Labor," *Representations* 83 (Summer 2003), p. 170.
25. Wright's earliest candlelight scene relates closely to Schalcken's penchant for attractive young women as models: *A Girl reading a Letter by Candlelight, with a Young Man looking over her Shoulder*, around 1762, oil on canvas, 88.9 × 69.8 cm, collection of Lt. Col. R.S. Nelthorpe; see Nicolson 1968, vol. 1, p. 239, no. 207. Nicolson downplays the connection to Schalcken, but does posit that Wright's method of staging light effects in an enclosed space in order to observe them likely derived from Schalcken's practice; see Nicolson 1968, vol. 1, pp. 47–48.
26. This conversation was reported by William Paulet Carey, in: *Letter to I…A…Esq., A Connoisseur, in London*, (Manchester: R. and W. Dean, 1809), p. 21; see Nicolson 1968, vol. 1, p. 85, who questions its accuracy, but underscores the critical view it conveys.
27. See Nicolson 1968, vol. 1, p. 237, no. 198; Egerton 1990, pp. 103–104, no. 50.
28. Nicolson 1968, vol. 1, p. 225, no. 268; Egerton 1990, pp. 174–175, no. 105.
29. Nicolson 1968, vol. 1, p. 247, no. 243; Egerton 1990, pp. 129–130, no. 67.
30. An example is his *Italian Landscape*, signed and dated 1790, oil on canvas, 103.5 × 130.4 cm, Washington: National Gallery of Art, Paul Mellon Collection (1983.1.47); see Nicolson 1968, vol. 1, p. 260, no. 292; Egerton 1990, pp. 190–191, no. 119.
31. Solkin posits that Wright's earlier blacksmith pictures reveal a suspicion for mere beauty, and an emphasis on the virtue and tempering character of labour, an attitude that appears to align with Burke's notions of the sublime; see Solkin 2003 (note 23, above), p. 184.
32. Joseph Wright of Derby, *The Corinthian Maid*, around 1782–5, oil on canvas, 106.3 × 130.8 cm, Washington: National Gallery of Art (1983.1.46); see Nicolson 1968, vol. 1, pp. 243–244, no. 224; Egerton 1990, pp. 132–134, no. 69.
33. See Nicolson 1968, vol. 1, p. 258, no. 283; Egerton 1990, pp. 164–165, no. 100.
34. Joseph Wright of Derby, *Antigonus in the Storm, Act III, scene iii, from Shakespeare's "The Winter's Tale"*, 1792, oil on canvas, 153.9 × 221.3 cm, Toronto: Art Gallery of Ontario (90/167); see Nicolson 1968, vol. 1, p. 245, no. 231.
35. Joseph Wright of Derby, *Romeo and Juliet. The Tomb Scene. 'Noise again! then I'll be brief'*, 1790, oil on canvas, 177.8 × 241.3 cm, Derby: Derby Museum and Art Gallery (1981-330); see Nicolson 1968, vol. 1, p. 245, no. 232; Egerton 1990, pp. 123–124, no. 63.
36. Letter from Judy Egerton to James Mundy, director of the Milwaukee Art Museum, 14 November 1986; photocopy in object file, Agnes Etherington Art Centre.
37. See Nicolson 1988, p. 745.
38. Wright to William Hayley, 22 December 1784; see Barker 2009, Letter 61.
39. Wright to William Hayley, 17 February 1785, London: National Portrait Gallery, in an extra-illustrated copy of Bemrose 1885; see Barker 2009, Letter 63.
40. Wright to William Hayley, 9 March 1783, Cambridge: Fitzwilliam Museum; see Bonehill 2008, p. 527 (not in Barker 2009).
41. See Barker 2009, p. 7 note 22: Barker estimates the height of the figures at 6–10 inches; the tallest, that of Curtis, is around 8 inches, others rise to around 2–3 inches, and the Spaniards in the water around 1 inch.
42. Philip James de Loutherbourg, *The Battle of the Nile*, 1800, oil on canvas, 152.4 × 214 cm, London: Tate Gallery (T01452).

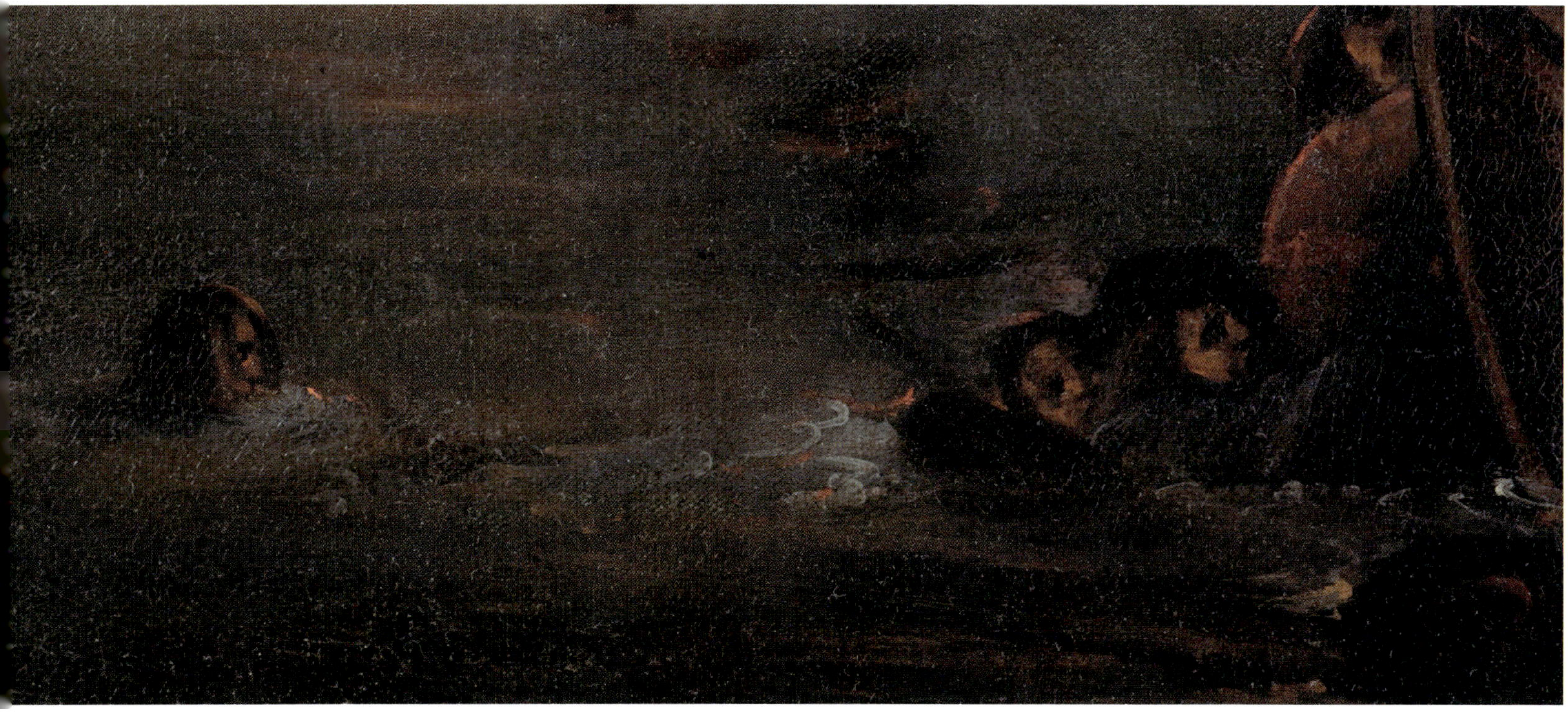

FROM COVENT GARDEN TO KINGSTON ONTARIO: A PICTURE'S PROVENANCE

JANET M. BROOKE

"**THE NAME OF JOSEPH WRIGHT OF DERBY**, once of high repute among English artists, has, during the last half-century and more sunk, altogether undeservedly, into a state of semi-oblivion." So wrote William Bemrose, in his extensive biography of Wright, published in 1885.[1] Indeed, Bemrose's magisterial effort, complete with meticulous transcriptions of manuscript and rare early printed sources, was the first monograph on the artist since his death in 1797. Another eighty years would pass before it was supplanted by Benedict Nicolson's authoritative catalogue raisonné of Wright's paintings, with little published of significance in the interim.[2]

The genesis of Joseph Wright of Derby's *A View of Gibraltar during the destruction of the Spanish Floating Batteries, on the 13th of September, 1782*, unknown to Nicolson beyond archival evidence at the time of his 1968 publication,[3] is described elsewhere in this catalogue. A reconstruction of the painting's provenance following its completion by Wright in 1785 to the present day is the subject of this essay. In a way, the history of *A View of Gibraltar* mirrors the fate of its creator, whose reputation, though substantial, failed even in his own day to reach the summit to which Wright aspired and that he believed he deserved. Following his death, it dimmed to a point that saw some of his pictures, such as this one, forgotten, attributed to others, or lost to the record.

Wright conceived his monumental *View of Gibraltar* with high ambitions: he deliberately chose both subject and scale to assert his artistic stature among his peers, and with his patrons and the viewing public. The painting commemorated a recent naval victory much in the news, and was part of the growing corpus of pictures depicting scenes from the celebrated event already completed, exhibited or underway by fellow artists.[4] In this first attempt to execute a grand battle-picture, Wright, at the age of fifty and often in delicate health, may well have overreached his natural skills and capacity, but as John Bonehill has pointed out here and elsewhere, the bold decision to create his *View of Gibraltar* was a tactical one, to be seen in the context of his break with the Royal Academy and the dearth of alternatives for public exposure. Wright executed *A View of Gibraltar* while he planned another ambitious, even radical, move: the display in London of twenty-four of his paintings, both unsold and borrowed from patrons, in a self-organized exhibition.[5] *A View of Gibraltar* was the centrepiece of the event, which opened, complete with a printed catalogue, in April 1785 in the rooms of the auctioneers Henry and John Robins at 9 and 10 Great Piazza, Covent Garden.[6]

Wright had great hopes for his new picture, confiding to his friend the poet William Hayley that he anticipated both "honour and profit" from the effort.[7] Envisaged early in 1783, it was barely completed in time for the exhibition, and was one of twelve works offered for sale. Described in the catalogue as the first of a pair (the second was never painted), it had been seen in Derby by Erasmus Darwin, who wrote Josiah Wedgwood on 14 January 1785: "Mr. Wright sais your pictures will scarcely be all finish'd for his exhibition. The Giberalter is indeed sublime."[8] Despite such praise, it remained unsold in January 1786, by which time Wright had spent several months eliciting help from friends to organize a raffle of the painting by subscription, calculating the sale of eighty tickets at 5 guineas each.[9] No such enterprise materialized, and by 12 April the picture was in the possession of John Milnes, who had agreed to pay £420 for it but who by then still owed the artist 200 guineas against the canvas.[10]

Debt notwithstanding, John Milnes, of Wakefield, West Yorkshire (1751–1810), was an enthusiastic patron, beginning with a portrait commission in 1776 (fig. 8).[11] By the time Milnes purchased Wright's large battle-picture ten years later, he owned at least ten of the artist's landscapes and literary subjects.[12] Perhaps Milnes stepped in to relieve a friend's financial burden: *A View of Gibraltar* had attracted limited attention beyond Wright's immediate circle during and after the exhibition and as the months passed, its chances of sale, by raffle or otherwise, diminished. It is no coincidence, surely, that the sale price to Milnes was equal to the amount Wright envisaged by the raffle, and the highest sum ever paid for a Wright during the artist's lifetime.

Milnes's patronage was part of a broader market for Wright's work in the emerging industrial centres west and north of Derbyshire, including Liverpool, where Wright resided from 1768 to 1771. He cultivated lifelong contacts and friends in the North West, among them Milnes, Wedgwood, Darwin and the print collector Daniel Daulby.[13] Milnes's family had resided in and around Wakefield, in West Yorkshire and

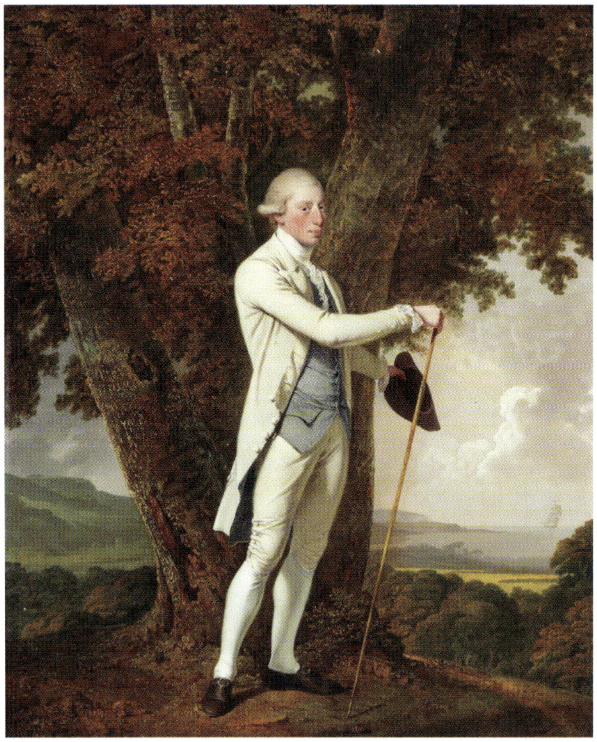

Fig. 8.
Joseph Wright of Derby
John Milnes
1776, oil on canvas, 127 × 101 cm
Paris, Musée du Louvre (RF1985-11)
Photo J. G. Berizzi

in Derbyshire for generations, with fortunes based in the cloth trade. His elder brother Robert Shore Milnes (around 1747–1837) sat for Wright in 1772.[14] The family's political sympathies were radical. John was in Paris from 1791 to 1792 with his mistress Catherine Carr (whom he later married); she bore him a son whom they named Alfred Mirabeau Washington Milnes (the middle names were understandably later dropped).[15]

In August 1797, the picture was seen in Wakefield and praised by the Rev. William Turner (1761–1859) in a paper read at the Literary and Philosophical Society, Newcastle upon Tyne: "The curious stranger, who has interest enough to obtain a sight of the house and paintings of Mr. John Milnes, will be particularly struck with the performances of that eminent artist, Mr. Wright of Derby. Here is the famous eruption of Mount Vesuvius; … and, above all, the destruction of the Spanish floating batteries at Gibraltar, which awfully displays his power to 'rule the element of fire.'"[16]

The Milnes family owned several distinguished properties in Wakefield, including Thornes House, newly built in 1779–1782 by the York architect John Carr, who may have worked also on additional Milnes homes.[17] Though commissioned by John Milnes's cousin James (1755–1805), Thornes House may have been the collection's location.[18] In any event, following James Milnes's death (and before John's), *A View of Gibraltar* was sold by the auctioneer Peter Coxe in 1806 with the contents of Egremont House, James Milnes's opulent London residence in Piccadilly. The painting was described in the catalogue as "deserving to be deposited in a National Gallery." An annotation shows the hammer price as a modest £71.8 and the buyer as "Smith."[19] No other Wrights were in the sale; by this time ownership of *A View of Gibraltar* appears to have passed from one cousin to another.

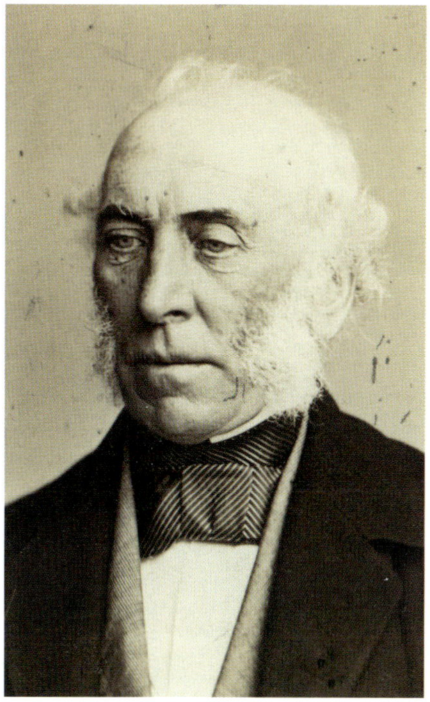

Fig. 9.
Vernon Heath
Samuel Jones Loyd,
1st Baron Overstone
albumen carte-de-visite, mid-1860s
London, National Portrait Gallery
(NPGAx29677)
© National Portrait Gallery, London

Whether "Smith" was a pseudonym or agent, we know that the actual buyer was the Liverpool-based picture dealer Thomas Vernon, who reported as much during a visit to Joseph Farington in London ten days after the sale, declaring that he would not re-sell the painting for less than 300 guineas.[20] Not much is known of Vernon's life or activities as a dealer; he seems to have been active between 1796 and 1821.[21] Though there is no archival evidence to suggest he knew Wright, they could well have met during Wright's years in Liverpool, where Vernon was a fixture as a dealer and auctioneer, selling, for example, Wright's friend Daniel Daulby's large collection of Rembrandt and other Old Master prints in 1799.[22] He acquired six small works at the sale of Wright's studio contents in 1801.[23] Vernon was bankrupt in 1816, and on 21 March his Old Master picture holdings went on the block.[24]

None of Vernon's Wrights, including *A View of Gibraltar*, were part of that sale. With few exceptions, the Wrights sold at the 1801 auction had not fetched more than a few pounds, including those purchased by Vernon. It seems that even by then, Wright's star was well on the wane. In any event, *A View of Gibraltar* slips from sight, reappearing several decades later in the picture collection of Samuel Jones Loyd, 1st Baron Overstone (1796–1883).

An eminent banker and financier, Overstone exercised considerable influence on the economic matters of the day, and was among Britain's wealthiest men. Elevated to the peerage in 1850, he ceased his formal banking activities. In the same year he was named a Trustee of the National Gallery, where he contributed actively to the debate around the acceptance and housing of the J.M.W. Turner and Robert Vernon bequests, and donated a large lunette fresco by Giulio Romano and Gianfrancesco Penni.[25] His love of art was longstanding and genuine, first reflected in his youthful letters home during his tour of the Continent in 1821, enthusing, especially, on sculpture, and again during a return visit to Rome in

1852, when he wrote in similar vein to a colleague: "I muse on these subjects [political woes in England] … until I become anxious and somewhat sad — But then I walk off to the Galleries of the Vatican — I walk amidst the ruins of the Forum and around the Coliseum by moonlight — I turn to the glorious Frescoes of M Angelo and of Raphael — and all is right again with me."[26] From early days he seems to have had little patience for what he called "the cant of connoisseurship,"[27] and at the National Gallery weighed in on thorny issues of authenticity, seeking opinions from experts.[28]

From the early 1830s at least, Overstone was also a significant collector of Old Master paintings.[29] In 1846, with Thomas Baring and Humphrey Mildmay, he acquired a number of important seventeenth century Dutch paintings from the prestigious Verstolk collection in The Hague,[30] and at his death his large collection included Dutch, French, Italian and British works, many of exceptional quality.

The first published record of Overstone's ownership of *A View of Gibraltar* appears in 1849, when he lent it to the annual British Institution exhibition.[31] In 1857, it was one of a large number of paintings he sent—including works by Perugino, Rembrandt, Steen, Claude, Murillo, Reynolds and Stubbs—to the famed *Art Treasures of the United Kingdom* exhibition held in Manchester, of which he was Chairman.[32] From around this time, we can begin to track the progressive decline in the picture's stature. In the exhibition's extensive official and press record, no mention is made of *A View of Gibraltar*—or rarely of Wright for that matter, who was additionally represented by several portraits.[33] In 1877, we find the picture hanging not in its owner's picture gallery, but in his billiard room at Overstone Park, his Northampton property, a residence inherited from his father in 1858 and grandly rebuilt in the early 1860s at the insistence of his wife. Overstone disliked the building and declined to occupy it, preferring to reside in his estate at Lockinge.[34] In 1921, following the death of his daughter and heir Lady Wantage, *A View of Gibraltar* still lingered at Overstone Park, by then relegated to a hall corridor, bereft of attribution and identity of subject and described simply as "a large gallery painting, Naval Battle Scene at Night (60-in by 102-in)," part of a local auction of the last goods and chattels of the family estate.[35]

The name of the painting's buyer was not recorded, but two years later, a picture of the same dimensions, representing the sortie at Gibraltar, appears in correspondence between Ehrich Galleries, New York, and the Illinois collector Nathaniel C. Sears. Ehrich Galleries, originally trading exclusively in Old Master paintings, was by the beginning of the twentieth century turning its attention increasingly to the growing American market for pictures by native sons, fielding exhibitions and auctions of, especially, early American portraits. On 7 August 1923, Harold Louis Ehrich apprised Sears that while recently in England, his brother and gallery partner Walter "came across" a picture "privately owned in England" that owing to its size "could be bought for a fraction of its real value," claiming it to be "one of the most important large subject pictures" of the Anglo-American painter John Singleton Copley. He offered it to Sears for $1800.[36]

The Honorable Sears (1854–1934), Chicago lawyer, and later judge and professor of law at Northwestern University, was an avid, if rather uneven, collector of American and Old Master paintings, to whom Ehrich Galleries sold a number of pictures over the years. He may or may not have known of Copley's large commission representing the Siege of Gibraltar for the Guildhall, London, but it is likely on that

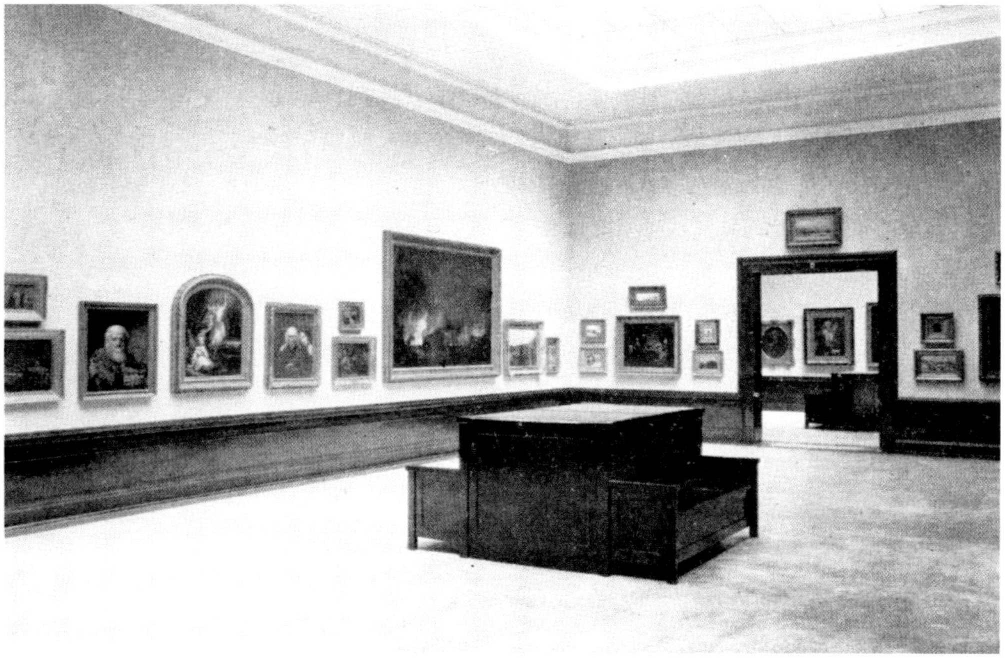

Fig. 10.
Interior view of the Sears Gallery, Elgin Academy, showing *A View of Gibraltar* on the left wall. From the 1926 edition of *Hilltop*, the Elgin Academy's yearbook

basis that Ehrich Galleries baptized its 1923 acquisition to that artist and represented it as such to Sears. The collector seems to have sought additional support for the attribution; in November 1923 the Philadelphia artist Albert Rosenthal reassured him that it was "big in design and in fine condition," and eventually on 5 June 1925 Ehrich forwarded Rosenthal's certificate of authenticity to Sears.[37] Its condition, however, was anything but fine. Indeed, the record also includes an invoice for the restoration of the painting at Ehrich Galleries before its departure to Illinois, this being the first of two aggressive interventions on the painting since its creation.[38]

By the early 1920s, Sears's acquisitions were made with a view to the donation of his collection to the Elgin Academy, a preparatory school chartered in 1839 on the outskirts of Chicago, so it is possible that the scale and heroic character of the picture's subject matter held special appeal. Opened in 1924, the Laura Davidson Sears Academy of Fine Arts (named for his wife) was a purpose-built gallery housing around 250 paintings; Sears's "Copley" is listed in successive editions of the gallery's catalogue, and illustrated in the inaugural publication.[39] A photograph in the 1926 edition of the school's yearbook, *Hilltop*, shows one of the Academy's large, elegantly wainscoted top-lit galleries, typical of North American museum architecture of the day, with *A View of Gibraltar* dominating a long wall (fig. 10).

By the 1960s, the Elgin Academy had abandoned its art gallery, and the fine neo-classical building was repurposed for more urgent pedagogical functions. A portion of the collection, including the battle picture ascribed to Copley, was deaccessioned in 1967, and sixty-five works were purchased by the Lenz Art Gallery, Milwaukee, in partnership with the Milwaukee collector Dr. Alfred Bader.

So began Bader's long and passionate association with *A View of Gibraltar*, which culminates in this publication. Offered for sale in a Lenz Art Gallery catalogue of the Sears Academy paintings in 1968, still under the attribution to Copley,[40] *A View of Gibraltar* remained unsold until 1973, when it was purchased by the Milwaukee Art Center (now Milwaukee Art Museum) through a gift from the Charleston Foundation in memory of its founder Paula Uihlein. Bader has elsewhere described the painting's fortune while at that institution.[41] De-accessioned in 2001 as by a Wright follower and stripped of its provenance as then known,[42] it was purchased by the Agnes Etherington Art Centre with funds provided by Bader. Convinced over these four decades that this canvas is indeed the picture Wright completed with high hopes in 1785, he has enthusiastically supported our research to document the painting and its history. Numerous factors—its compromised condition and altered character primary among them—have conspired to sink the painting into undeserved oblivion. Its virtually unbroken provenance here elaborated offers compelling evidence towards repositioning it into Wright's oeuvre.

1. See Bemrose 1885, p. v.
2. See Nicolson 1968.
3. Ibid., no. 245. On Nicolson's later examination and attribution of the picture, see the essay by David de Witt in this catalogue.
4. Including George Carter (1784, National Army Museum, London), William Hamilton (1783), James Jefferys (1783, Government Art Collection, London), Dominic Serres (four views, 1784–1792), Francis Swaine (1782), Lamarr West (RA 1783) and Thomas Whitcombe (1783, Milwaukee Art Museum). John Singleton Copley's 1783 commission for the Guildhall, London was completed in 1791. Other pictures completed after Wright's include canvases by the American John Trumbell, in three versions of *The Sortie Made by the Garrison of Gibraltar* executed between 1786 and 1789 (Cincinnati Art Museum, Cincinnati OH; Corcoran Gallery, Washington DC; and Metropolitan Museum of Art NY).
5. See Bonehill 2008.
6. See Hayley 1785.
7. Wright to William Hayley, 13 January 1783; see Barker 2009, Letter 45.
8. Desmond King-Hele, ed. *The Collected Letters of Erasmus Darwin* (Cambridge: Cambridge University Press, 2007), p. 238. Among the other then-unfinished pictures to which Darwin alluded are *The Lady in Milton's Comus* (Nicolson 1968, no. 234; Walker Art Centre, Liverpool), *The Corinthian Maid* (Nicolson 1968, no. 224; National Gallery of Art, Washington DC) and *Penelope Unravelling her Web, by Lamp-light* (Nicolson 1968, no. 225; J. Paul Getty Museum, Malibu), nos. 1, 13 and 14 in the 1785 catalogue (see note 6 above). The reference suggests that Darwin, erroneously, may have thought *A View of Gibraltar* was also intended for Wedgwood. Darwin was sufficiently impressed to allude to it in the 1790 and subsequent editions of *The Loves of the Plants* (London: J. Johnson, 1790), p. 20.
9. As recorded in two letters from Wright to his friend the Liverpool collector Daniel Daulby, 14 November 1785 and 14 January 1786; see Barker 2009, Letters 67 and 68. In Letter 67, Wright proposed the sale of eighty tickets at 3 guineas each; in Letter 68 he revised the price to 5 guineas.
10. Wright to William Hayley 12 April 1786: "I have disposed of my picture of Gibraltar for 420 Gns [sic. pounds?] to a private Gent.^{n} wch will spare me many an awkward sensation excited by the idea of having it raffled for" (see Barker 2009, Letter 71). See also Barker 2009, Account Book, fols. 61^{r}–62^{v}: "Mem.^{d} – 15th Sep.^{tr}, 1787 – Remains to be paid to me by Mr John Milnes, on account of the picture of Gibraltar, two hundred guineas, and by right [he] ought to pay the Int.^{r} of that money from the time he has withheld the commission from me to replace two other pictures in the room of the two he has of Vesuvius and the Gerandolo."
11. Wright recorded the completion of the commission in a letter to his brother Richard Wright on 8 May 1776; see Barker 2009, Letter 28. It is possible they had met earlier; see Barker 2009, Letter 15 (13 April 1774), in which Wright asks his sister Nancy to "inquire of Miles" for possible purchasers for his *Old Man and Death* (see Nicolson 1968, no. 220), exhibited at the Society of Artists that year. The same misspelling of the surname appears in Barker 2009, Letter 20. Egerton 1990, pp. 68–69 correctly notes the sitter is not the John Milnes identified by Nicolson 1968, under no. 107 as the sitter's father (1710–1771).
12. As listed in Egerton 1990, under p. 69, no. 27, and Wright's Account Book; see Barker 2009, Account book, fols. 19^{r}, 19^{v}, 53^{r}, 59^{v}, 61^{r}, 62^{v}, 66^{v}. Milnes continued to buy Wright's pictures until at least 1791; see Barker 2009, Letter 108 to John Leigh Phillips, 20 May 1791: "I have just finished for Mr Milnes another picture." An *Ugolino* is cited in Turner 1797 (note 16 below).
13. On this period and its impact on Wright's career, see Elizabeth E. Barker and Alex Kidson, *Joseph Wright of Derby in Liverpool*, exhib. cat. (Liverpool: Walker Art Gallery; and New Haven and London: Yale University Press, 2007).
14. See Nicolson 1968, no. 107. New York, Sotheby's, 25 January 2007, no. 69, purchased by the dealer Jean-Luc Baroni for an American buyer. Coincidentally, Robert Shore Milnes served as lieutenant governor of Lower Canada 1797–1808. Rather more remarkably, we learn from William Betham, *The Baronetage of England; or, the History of the English Baronets, and such Baronets of Scotland as are of English Families…, vol. V: Supplementary* (London: Warde and Betham, 1805), p. 460, that John Milnes also seems to have sojourned in Lower Canada—presumably at his brother's official residence in Quebec City—in 1805.
15. John Chapple, *Elizabeth Gaskell: The Early Years* (Manchester/New York: Manchester University Press, 1997), p. 91. I thank Annabel Hanson for this reference.
16. Rev. William Turner, "Observations on a tour through parts of York and Lancashire, read August 8th, 1797," collated in "Papers read at the Monthly Meetings, 1793–1814," Newcastle upon Tyne, Literary and Philosophical Society (N800/1), vol. 2; published by "V.F." in *The Monthly Magazine* 4 (September 1797), pp. 173–177. Other than the *Vesuvius* and *Gibraltar*, Turner cites a *Girandolo* ("fire works"), "Dr. Beattie's Edwin, Sterne's Captive, Count Ugolino, &c."

17. Paul Breman and Denise Addis, *Guide to Vitruvius Britannicus: An Annotated and Analytic Index to the Plates* (New York: Blom, 1972), p. 27. Thornes House was converted to a school in 1921, and destroyed by fire in 1951. I am grateful to Annabel Hanson for her research on the Milnes family properties in Wakefield.

18. James and John Milnes were related through their grandfathers John and Robert Milnes, who were brothers. Egerton 1990, p. 69 suggested that John Milnes's collection was housed in an unnamed family property at Wakefield "with a picture gallery seventy feet long," whose contents were sold in 1808, with no surviving documentation. The ground floor plan of Thornes House published in 1802 (George Richardson, *The New Vitruvius Britannicus* [London: Bulmer, 1802; repr. New York, Blom, 1970], pl. 51) shows no such gallery. No image or plan of the upper floor is known.

19. London, Piccadilly, Egremont House, 16 June 1806, no. 60; see Getty Provenance Index Br-427. "Smith" is further identified in an annotation as residing "N9 [or 19] Broad Street Back of RI Exchange." Another annotated copy of the same catalogue deemed the picture "w[ort]h 500 G[n]s," while a third supplies approximate dimensions that likely included the frame. Information concerning James Milnes is sparse. According to Burke's *Landed Gentry*, he was MP for Bletchingley (Surrey); his fortune was considerably enlarged through his marriage to Mary Ann Busk. They had no issue. Egremont House, later called Cambridge House (94 Piccadilly at Half Moon Street), built in 1756 by the 2nd Earl of Egremont, was sold to Milnes by 1794. It was subsequently occupied by the 1st Marquess of Cholmondeley (1820s) and from 1829 by the 1st Duke of Cambridge, and Lord Palmerston (1855–1865) before being acquired by the Royal and Military (In and Out) Club. It is now privately owned.

20. Joseph Farington, *The Diary of Joseph Farington*, ed. Kathryn Cave, vol. 7 (New Haven/London: Yale University Press, 1982), p. 2797: "Vernon told me that at the sale of the late Mr. John Mill's [sic] pictures at Egremont House Piccadilly, He bought *Wright's picture of the destruction of the floating batteries off Gibraltar* for 68 guineas. – Mr. Mills gave Wright 500 guineas [sic] for it. – Vernon will not, He says, sell it for less than 300 gs" (entry for 26 June 1806).

21. According to the Getty Provenance Index Br-1372. According to Barker and Kidson 2007 (see note 13), p. 214, he was active 1776–1813. See also C. P. Darcy, *The Encouragement of the Fine Arts in Lancashire 1760–1860*, Remains Historical and Literary Connected with the Palatine Counties of Lancaster and Chester, vol. 24, Third Series (Manchester: Manchester University Press for The Chetham Society, 1976), pp. 127, 139.

22. Liverpool, T. Vernon, *A Catalogue of Drawings, Prints,…and Books, Belonging to the Late Daniel Daulby…Consisting of the Works of the Most Celebrated Masters…, Particularly of a Most Extensive and Valuable Collection of the Works of Rembrandt, which will be sold by…T. Vernon, in his Great Room, in Marble-Street.* 12 [–21] August 1799; Getty Provenance Index Br-A5749.

23. London, Christie's, 6 May 1801, nos. 2 ("A View of the Lakes"), 14 ("A small pleasing View of a Harbour by Moonlight, and an unfinished Landscape, the Companion"), 18 ("An Italian Landscape with Ruin"), 20 ("A View of the Ponte Nomentano, near Rome, unfinished"), 24 ("The Glass-House, a Sketch") and 43 ("An upright View in the Convent of the Latomie at Syracuse").

24. Bath, Horatio Thurston (The Auction Room), *Mr. Thos. Vernon, a Bankrupt*, 21 March 1816, 45 lots; Getty Provenance Index Br-1372.

25. Lord Overstone, *The Correspondence of Lord Overstone*, ed. D. P. O'Brien, vol. 1 (Cambridge: Cambridge University Press, 1971), pp. 33–34. The donated painting is *Saint Mary Magdalene borne by Angels*, 1520–1521, inv. NG225.

26. Overstone 1971, vol. 2, p. 527, Letter 263: Overstone to C. Wood, 2 February 1852.

27. Overstone 1971, vol. 1, p. 18, Letter 15: Overstone, from Florence to his mother, 29 September 1821.

28. Overstone 1971, vol. 3, p. 1175: Overstone to G. W. Norman. The paintings in question were *Christ Blessing the Little Children* then ascribed to Rembrandt, Correggio's *Ecce Homo* and Michelangelo's *Entombment*.

29. For example, in 1832 he purchased Murillo's large *Virgin and Child*, 1670–1672, now in the Metropolitan Museum of Art, NY.

30. Mike Weaver, *Whisper of the Muse: The Overstone Album and Other Photographs by Julia Margaret Cameron* (Malibu: The J. Paul Betty Museum, 1986), p. 18.

31. London, British Institution, *Pictures by Italian, Spanish, Flemish, Dutch, French and English Masters*, Summer 1849, p. 13, no. 117 (as "The Sortie of Gibraltar"). See also: Algernon Graves, *A Century of Loan Exhibitions 1813–1912*, vol. 4 (London: A. Graves, 1914), p. 1717.

32. *Catalogue of the Art Treasures of the United Kingdom Collected at Manchester in 1857* (London: Bradbury and Evans, 1857), no. 81. Overstone replaced the Earl of Ellsemere, who died shortly before the exhibition's opening.

33. Thus, for example, in *A Handbook of the Gallery of British Painting in the Art Treasures Exhibition* (London: Bradbury and Evans, 1857), reprinting the succession of articles by Tom Taylor in *The Manchester Guardian* describing the exhibition over the course of its presentation, Wright's name is absent, while all other British artists included in the exhibition—from Reynolds, West and Gainsborough to Northcote, Hudson and Opie—merit a detailed biography and description of the many hundreds of works on view.

34. *Descriptive Catalogue of the Pictures at Overstone Park*, 1877, p. 10, no. 14.

35. London, Curtis and Henson, *Overstone Park, Northampton*, 31 January – 3 February 1921, no. 982. I am grateful to James Mulraine for locating a copy of this catalogue. Overstone Park was subsequently converted to a school, and later a church. It was gutted by fire in 2001.

36. Photocopy of letter in object file, Agnes Etherington Art Centre.

37. Photocopies of an undated letter postmarked 13 November 1923 and certificate in object file, Agnes Etherington Art Centre.

38. Photocopy of invoice dated 7 November 1923 from Ehrich Galleries in object file, Agnes Etherington Art Centre. This and the documents cited in notes 36–37 were first published by Erdmann 1974, p. 270 note 3. The treatment history of the painting is outlined in Barbara Klempan's essay in this publication.

39. *Catalogue of the Laura Davidson Sears Academy of Fine Arts, Elgin Academy and Junior College* (Elgin: Elgin Academy, 1924), pp. 8–9.

40. Milwaukee, Lenz Art Gallery, *American Paintings from the Collection of the Laura Davidson Sears Academy of Fine Arts of the Elgin Academy, Elgin, Illinois*, 1968, no. 11.

41. Alfred Bader, "Lost Masterpieces and Happy Endings," *Queen's Quarterly*, 114, no. 1 (Spring 2007), pp. 97–108.

42. New York, Christie's East, *Old Master Paintings*, 10 October 2001, no. 46.

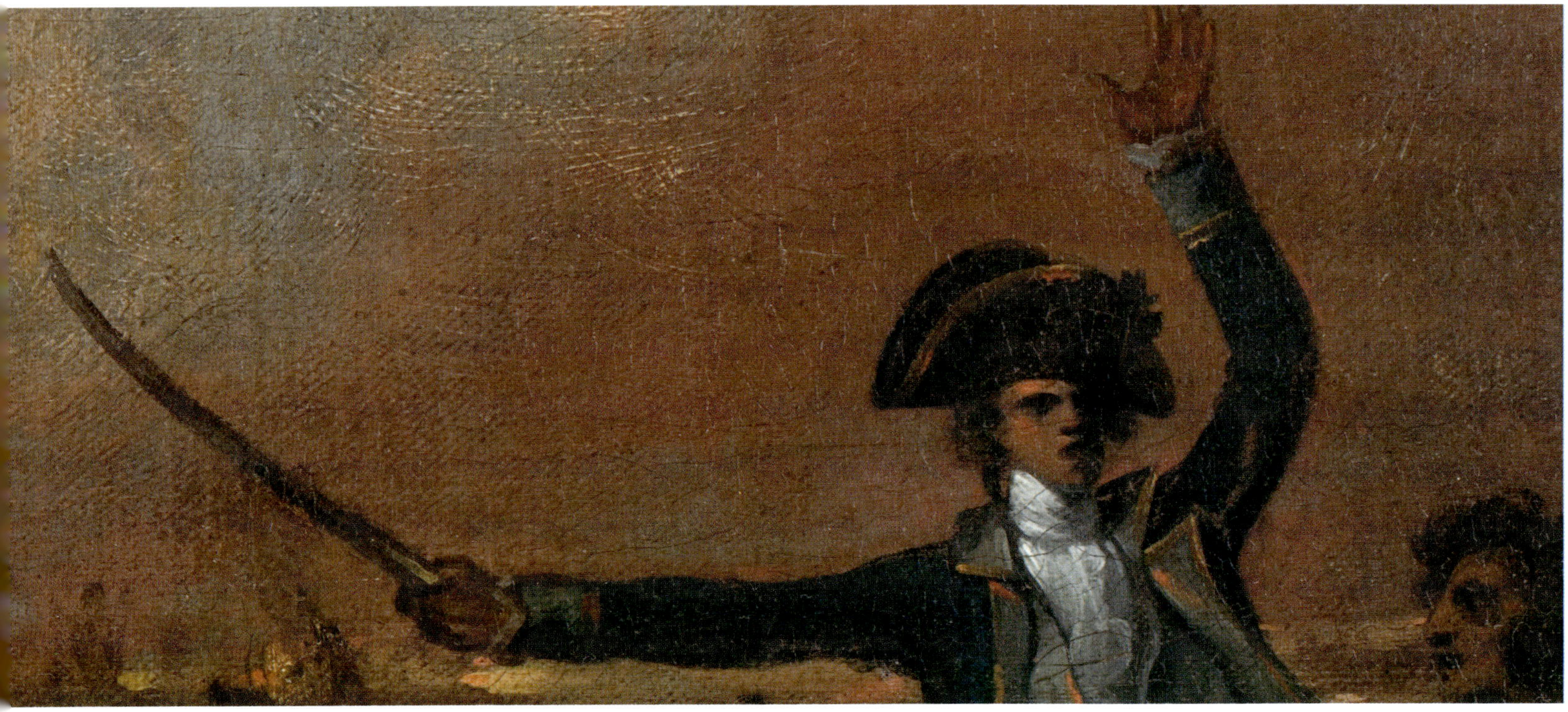

TECHNICAL EXAMINATION AND CONSERVATION TREATMENT OF *A VIEW OF GIBRALTAR*

BARBARA KLEMPAN

THE TECHNICAL EXAMINATION of *A View of Gibraltar during the destruction of the Spanish Floating Batteries, on the 13th of September, 1782* and subsequent conservation treatment spanned a four year period between 2003 and 2007. The project presented many challenges due to the deteriorated condition of the painting and initial questionable attribution to Joseph Wright of Derby. Working closely with the Director and Bader Curator of European Art at the Agnes Etherington Art Centre, the Canadian Conservation Institute and scientists within the Art Conservation Program at Queen's University, we collected valuable scientific and technical information on the painting's general structure and condition, the painting techniques and the history of previous conservation treatments. As the actual treatment got underway, specific information on the artist's technique and materials was revealed, such as the use of dead-colouring, along with additional stylistic and historical information, all of which supported the final attribution of the painting to Joseph Wright of Derby. This was a project that clearly united the disciplines of art history, art conservation and conservation science.

INITIAL EXAMINATION AND HISTORICAL RECORDS OF PREVIOUS TREATMENTS

Our initial examination of *A View of Gibraltar* occurred at the Agnes Etherington Art Centre in 2003. We observed that the piece was painted on a large, single flax canvas of twill weave which was mounted to a modern wood stretcher with two vertical cross bars and one horizontal cross bar. The painted surface was uneven, with raised and depressed areas caused by previously restored tears and old linings, and it was covered in layers of thickly discoloured overpaint and varnish. A large, carved gilt frame surrounded the painting. Records showed that the painting had been restored at least twice in the twentieth century, once in 1923[1] and again in 1972.[2] Of particular interest was the last recorded restoration in 1972 by Mary D. Randall, a painting restorer with a studio on Lansdowne Road, London.[3] Dr. Alfred Bader sent the painting to her from Milwaukee, Wisconsin for treatment. Art historian Benedict Nicolson examined the painting while it was at Randall's studio and wrote to Bader:

> As you realise it is a wreck and Mrs. Randall is not even able to get off all the overpainting without making it seem even worse of a wreck. She has in my opinion done what she could humanly do, and will now cover up the worst areas of paint losses. Fortunately some of the groups of sailors and officers in the foreground gunboats are sufficiently well preserved to look like Wrights, and the general composition is still impressive. She is proposing to eliminate the outside strips to left and right which are later than the painting, and to restretch it.[4]

There is some indication that Randall applied the most recent lining canvas to the back of the work in addition to the cleaning.[5] We made numerous attempts to find information on Randall's practice in London, including a request in *The Picture Restorer*.[6] To date, no further information about her practice has come to light.

SCIENTIFIC AND TECHNICAL EXAMINATION

In 2003, the painting underwent a rigorous scientific and technical examination at the Canadian Conservation Institute in Ottawa to provide us with a record of the materials and techniques used by the artist.[7] At the time of the examination, the attribution of the painting to Joseph Wright of Derby was in question and we felt that a technical examination might reveal painting characteristics unique to this artist's work. The painting was recorded through photography, x-radiography, ultraviolet fluorescence photography and infrared reflectography.

The examination showed several interesting characteristics of the work. The radiograph clearly indicated that the original canvas had a twill weave, a typical canvas material used by Wright in the 1780s.[8] A technical analysis of forty-eight oil paintings firmly attributed to Wright by paintings conservator Rica Jones confirmed the artist's use of twill canvas as a support.[9] Jones's essay also included detailed information on Wright's grounds, binding media and pigments, and was an invaluable comparative tool when examining materials from *A View of Gibraltar*.

The radiograph further revealed that all four edges of the canvas were cut down with no tacking margins present. However, it also showed that there was garlanding along the upper edge (approximately 8

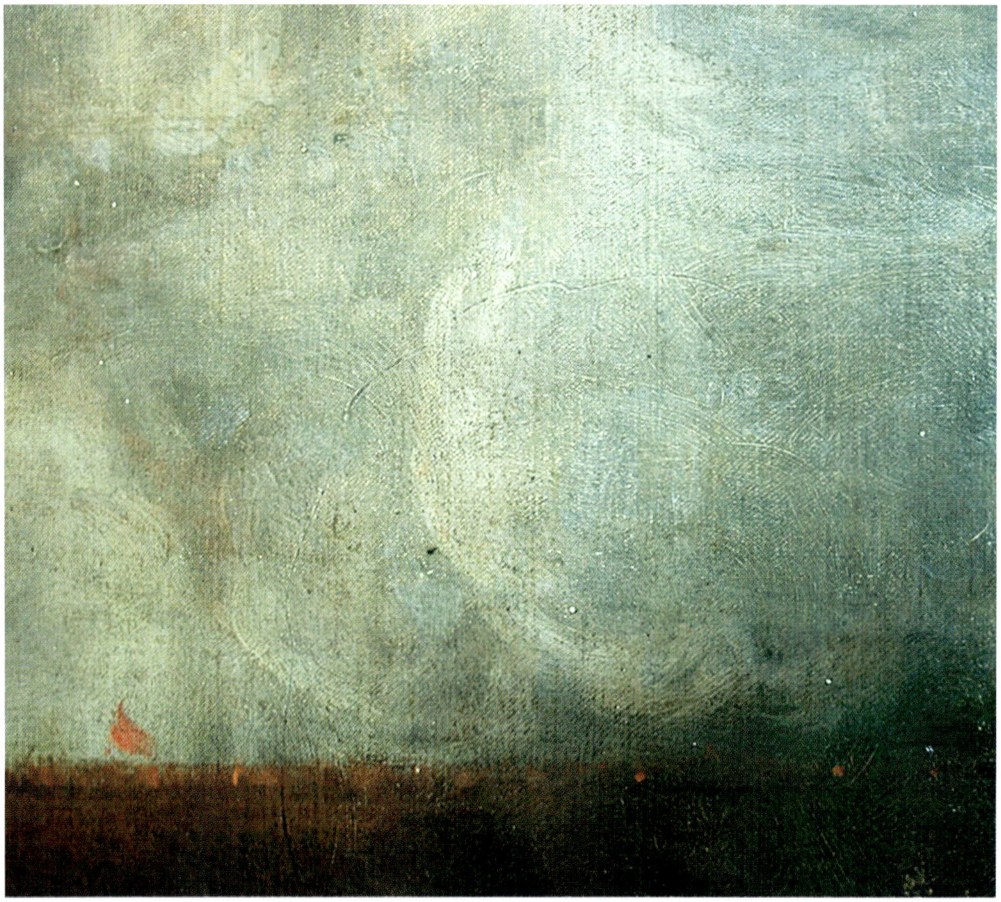

Fig. 11. Detail of incised lines in wet paint made with the blunt end of a paintbrush, before varnish removal

centimetres into the painting) and there was some evidence of original folded canvas that indicated that this top edge was the original fold-over edge. Additional garlanding along the bottom edge (approximately 5 centimetres into the painting) clearly indicated that these edges were not cut down as much as the right and left edges, which exhibited no garlanding.[10] Exact measurements of the paint film, taken with a microscope, established that the painting was 158.8 centimetres high and 235.0 centimetres wide. If we presume that the garlanding was the same on the top and bottom edge (8 centimetres into the work) it would add 3 centimetres to the total height dimension thus making it 161.3 centimetres high. This height measurement closely matches an 1877 catalogue entry for a painting identified as Wright's *Siege of Gibraltar* at Overstone Park, where the measurements were given as 64 inches high and 105 inches wide (162.5 centimetres by 266.7 centimetres.)[11] Since there was no garlanding present along the right or left sides of the work, it was not possible to calculate the original width of the painting.

Incised lines in the area of clouds along the right side of the painting were also visible on the radiographs. The artist likely made these with the blunt end of a paintbrush in wet paint to reveal the underlying paint film, a technique used by Wright, according to Rica Jones (fig. 11).[12] The radiographs also indicated a network of fine age cracks throughout the surface and that the paint film was generally thinly applied. Microscopic examination of the paint layers also supported these observations (fig. 12). Numerous tears and paint losses were clearly visible on the x-ray.

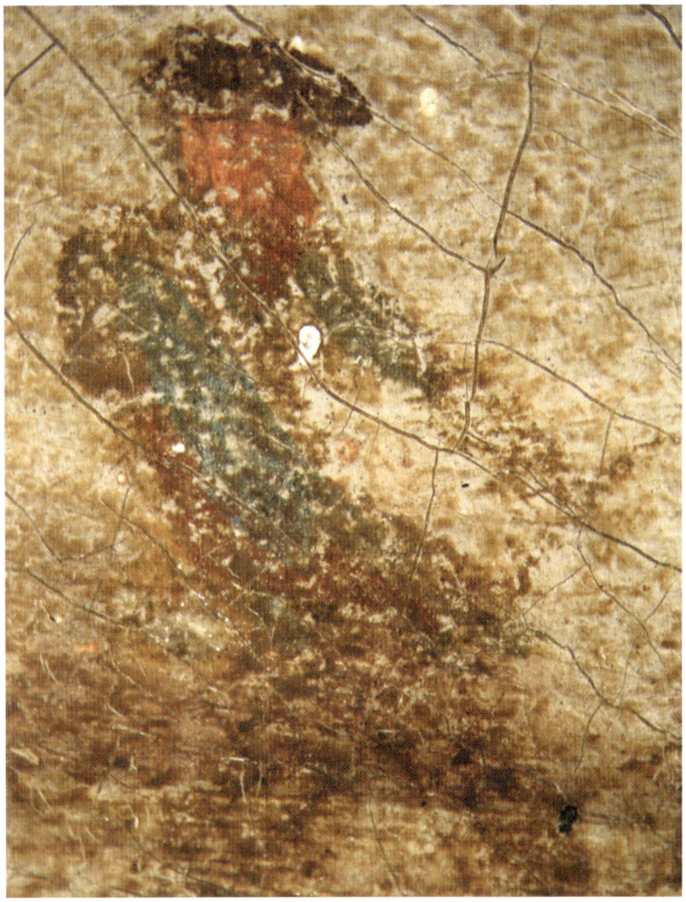

Fig. 12. Detail of fine network of cracks in paint film before varnish removal

Ultraviolet fluorescence photography, also undertaken during the initial examination of the painting, showed an unevenly varnished surface with at least two distinguishable layers of overpaint and a very thick, unevenly applied varnish. The use of ultraviolet light to examine a painting is commonly used by painting conservators to reveal otherwise invisible information about varnish layers and previous treatments such as overpainting. Infrared reflectography did not reveal underdrawing or other information relating to the artist's technique.[13]

Scientific examination of *A View of Gibraltar* by the Canadian Conservation Institute included taking samples of ground, paint layers, medium and varnish. The white ground found on the work was identified as a mixture of lead white, lead carbonate and calcium carbonate in drying oil.[14] According to Rica Jones's study, Wright used brilliant white grounds from the mid-1760s onwards and most of these grounds were composed of the lead white mixture mentioned above.[15] The paint layers sampled by conservation scientists at the Canadian Conservation Institute were complex mixtures of various pigments such as bone black, iron oxide, lead white, Naples yellow, Prussian blue, vermilion and an organic brown, possibly Vandyke brown.[16] Cross-sections showed the use of dead-colouring, a technique used by Wright whereby a coloured sketch layer is placed over a white ground.[17] In the case of *A View of Gibraltar*, various cross-sections revealed the following: a green dead colour in an area of the water; a brown dead colour in the yellowish part of the sky on the left hand side; and a greenish-beige dead

Fig. 13. Detail of pitted and flattened paint film from linings, before varnish removal

colour near the horizon in an area of the clouds.[18] The conservation scientists established that the binding media was linseed oil, typical for this period.[19] They also identified the upper layers of varnish as a cyclohexanone resin, likely a modern ketone resin, applied during the 1972 restoration campaign. Further testing of earlier varnish layers found beneath the cyclohexanone resin revealed that they were mixtures of linseed oil and a mastic and Pinaceae resin, such as colophony.[20]

Analyses of additional components of the painting were performed at Queen's University's Art Conservation Program to assist with understanding the structure of the painting during conservation treatment. The painting had been lined twice in the past with flax canvases of a plain weave[21] and both linings were adhered with a mixture of glue (protein) and starch adhesive.[22] As previously mentioned, Mary Randall applied the last lining in 1972. These linings caused irreparable damage to the original paint film. Excessive heat and pressure during the lining process caused the texture of the original canvas to be imprinted onto the paint film, and also resulted in a pitted and flattened surface in some areas of the painting (fig. 13). The lining process was likely undertaken to support two large, tent-shaped tears in the canvas that can be clearly seen on the x-ray. The painting may have fallen onto a sharp-edged object, such as a table or chair, causing the tears. The linings, however, were in good condition and required only minor repairs along the edges and corners.

TREATMENT OF *A VIEW OF GIBRALTAR*

The examinations of *A View of Gibraltar* and the resulting scientific and technical information provided

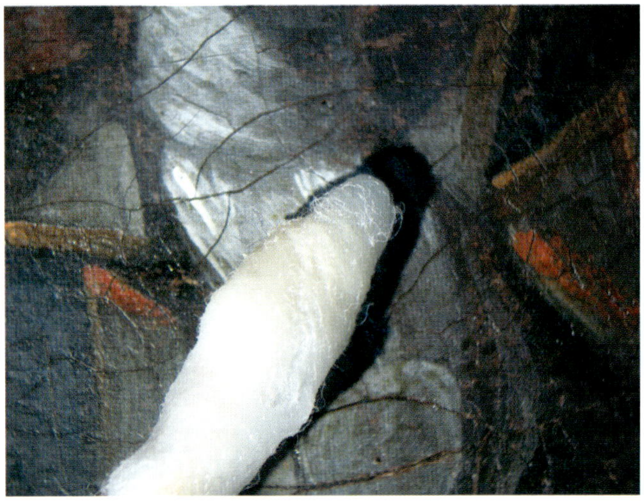

Fig. 14. Removal of discoloured varnish layers

a framework for discussions with the Director and Curator of the Agnes Etherington Art Centre to formulate a treatment protocol. We opted for a mainly aesthetic treatment, since the original paint was not actively flaking or otherwise visibly deteriorated. The main objective in treating the surface was to remove the discoloured varnish and extensive retouching from the 1972 restoration campaign. Ultraviolet examination had already provided details on the possibility of at least two thick layers of overpaint covering much of the sky area. Removal of these layers could reveal the artist's original brush strokes and further contribute to a determination of the painting's authorship. It could also, however, reveal a thin and abraded original surface, which would prohibit further cleaning. We decided to proceed with the cleaning in a series of well-defined stages that would be evaluated periodically and altered if required.

The first stage of the conservation treatment was surface cleaning to remove superficial grime with cotton swabs and an aqueous cleaning agent. The swabs picked up a greyish-yellow film from the surface that was identified by FTIR (Fourier transform infrared spectroscopy) as natural oil.[23] This oily layer could have come from an "oiling out" process that provides temporary saturation of the paint film, often used by galleries or art dealers prior to an exhibition or sale, or from environmental pollutants. Following the surface cleaning, we undertook extensive testing to find solvents that would remove the ketone resin varnish from the surface without damaging the paint layers. An alcohol-based mixture was selected to remove both the ketone resin varnish and any earlier varnish residue and thick overpaint (fig. 14).

We began the removal process by working in small areas, starting along the far right side of the painting. If the overpaint in this area covered severely abraded or damaged paint, we had the option of halting the cleaning process and re-examining the conservation protocol. The cleaning, in fact, revealed a worn but aesthetically pleasing surface. Design elements not previously seen through the thick overpaint in the area of the fortifications were now visible and this greatly added to our understanding of the painter's technique. An overall brown dead colour was applied over the white ground, and the fortifications were painted directly over the smoke clouds using spontaneous brushwork and a vigorous scumbling[24] of a more opaque dark brown paint over a red-brown paint (fig. 15). The dark brown centres of the smoke clouds were added after the lighter rims had been painted. In the white smoke clouds, light grey paint

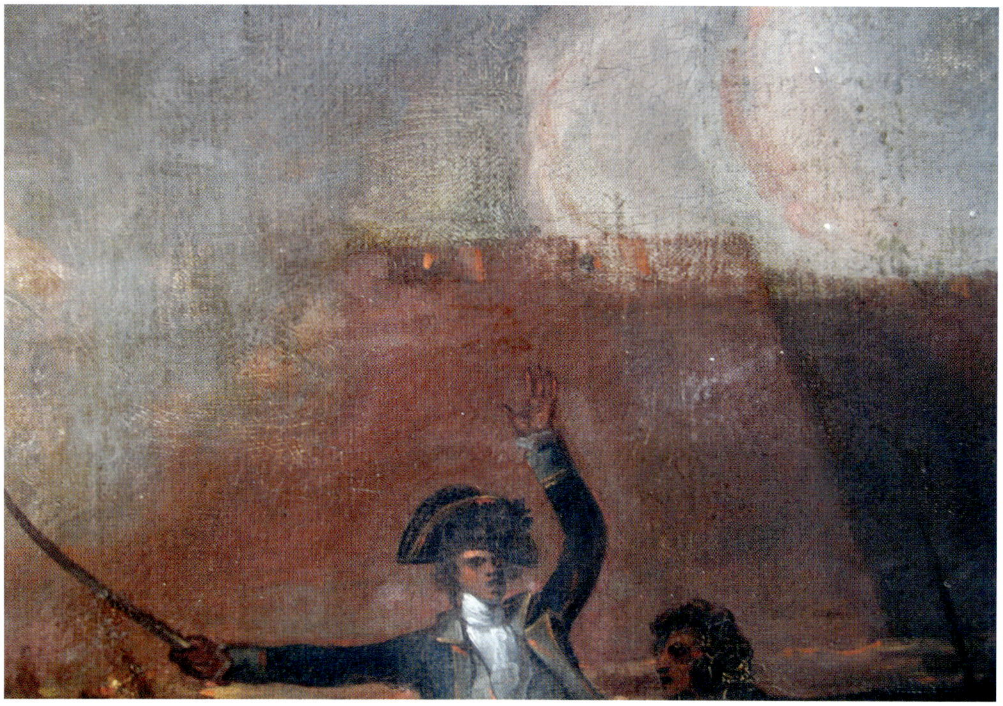

Fig. 15. Detail of fortifications showing scumbling of brown paint and underlying clouds, during varnish removal

was applied first, followed by pink highlights and a dark pink border. The sky area in the upper right did not appear to use dead-colouring, and consisted of dark blue-green paint applied over the white ground, followed by brown paint.

As the cleaning proceeded towards the central area of the work, previous damage to the painting became apparent. The most notable areas of mechanical damage were in the centre and left of centre, where the canvas had been torn in the past. Once we removed the discoloured varnish and thick overpaint from these areas, the true extent of the damages became apparent. The tears were wide but stable, with no evidence of planar distortion. Other areas of the painting exhibited severe surface abrasion and paint loss. One such area was along the far left edge near the centre, which first appeared to be a flat diagonal form covered in dark brown overpaint. Very little original paint remained beneath the overpaint, but the cleaning revealed an irregularly shaped object that may have been the remnants of an unfurling sail. The ropes of the sail were clearly visible beneath the shape and there was a slight indication of a diagonal beam holding the sail. Computer graphics, using false colour,[25] revealed a faint image of the sail (fig. 16). The resultant image assisted in reconstructing the sail during inpainting.

Once we completed the cleaning, old fills were either mechanically removed or repaired with a fill material composed of animal glue and calcium carbonate. Fills were toned with watercolour and the surface was brush varnished with a non-yellowing acrylic coating. Inpainting was undertaken with acrylic resin medium and dry pigments. We consulted periodically with the Director and Curator of the Agnes Etherington Art Centre during the inpainting stage, as it was of great importance to retain as much original design as possible and restrict inpainting to only those areas that had previous paint loss due to mechanical damage. Once this stage was complete, the surface was sprayed with a non-yellowing acrylic varnish.

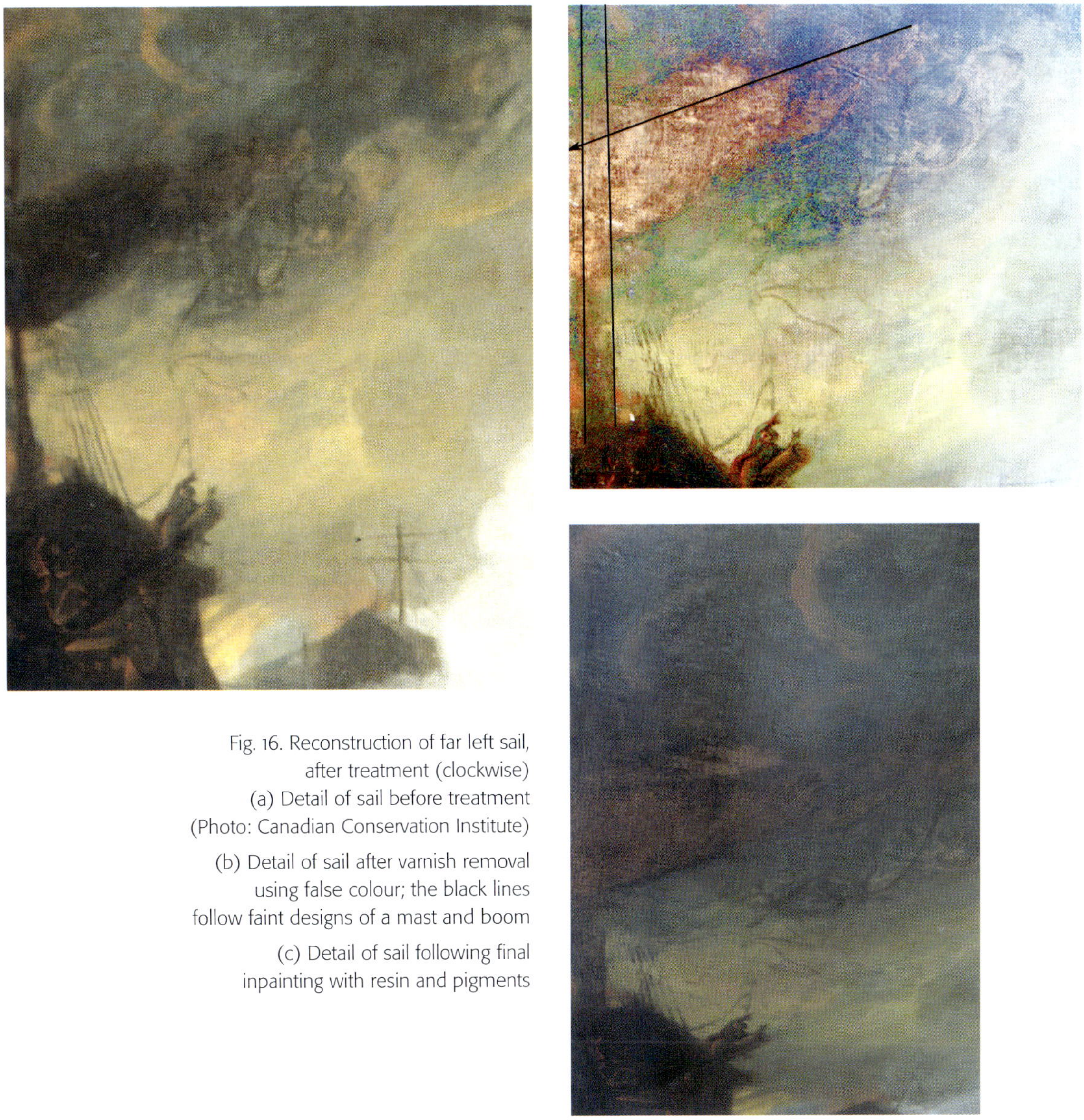

Fig. 16. Reconstruction of far left sail, after treatment (clockwise)
(a) Detail of sail before treatment (Photo: Canadian Conservation Institute)
(b) Detail of sail after varnish removal using false colour; the black lines follow faint designs of a mast and boom
(c) Detail of sail following final inpainting with resin and pigments

CONCLUDING REMARKS

A View of Gibraltar has withstood over two centuries of changing ownership, restorations and the perils of overseas travel, but it has yielded substantial technical information to help establish its final attribution to Joseph Wright of Derby. The poor surface condition of the painting undoubtedly contributed to initial questions of attribution and the double lining prevented a visual inspection of the original canvas, which can help date a work of art. The severely overpainted and heavily varnished surface also prevented detailed stylistic examination of the work. With the use of modern scientific examination techniques and equipment, it has been possible to identify the many components of this painting. Radiography revealed the canvas structure, incised marks in the paint, painterly style and general physical state of paint and ground layers. Ultraviolet examination displayed the uneven thickness of the varnish layers and identified areas of extensive overpainting. Cross-sections indicated a systematic build up of paint layers, including the use of dead-colouring, and confirmed the use of Wright's typical paint palette as established by Rica Jones. The scientific and technical examination of this work and subsequent treatment has led us to a new appreciation and understanding of this formerly unattributed work.

1. Photocopy of letter from Ehrich Galleries, New York to the Elgin Academy, Illinois, pertaining to the restoration of "Siege of Gibraltar," 7 November 1923, Agnes Etherington Art Centre object file.
2. Photocopy of letter from Benedict Nicolson to Dr. Alfred Bader concerning the restoration treatment of *A View of Gibraltar* in London, 28 January 1972, Agnes Etherington Art Centre object file.
3. Ibid.
4. Ibid.
5. See Erdmann 1974, pp. 270–273.
6. Barbara Klempan, "Request for Information on Restoration Treatment," *The Picture Restorer*, no. 32 (Autumn 2007), p. 25.
7. Kate Helwig and Jeremy Powell, "Scientific Examination of a Painting Attributed to Joseph Wright of Derby (Part 1)," Analytical Research Laboratory, Canadian Conservation Institute, unpublished report, 2003 (ARL 4148).
8. See Jones 1990, pp. 263–271.
9. Ibid.
10. The importance of garlanding on canvases cannot be overstated since the pattern can indicate where the canvas was tacked to a stretcher frame. These garlands can help determine the original size of the picture's surface.
11. *Descriptive Catalogue of the Pictures at Overstone Park*, 1877, p. 10, no. 14.
12. See Jones 1990, p. 270.
13. Helwig and Powell 2003 (see note 7).
14. Kate Helwig, Jennifer Poulin and Jeremy Powell, "Scientific Examination of a Painting Attributed to Joseph Wright of Derby (Part 3)," Analytical Research Laboratory, Canadian Conservation Institute, unpublished report, 2007 (ARL 4148.3), p. 17.
15. See Jones 1990, p. 263.
16. Helwig, Poulin and Powell 2007 (see note 14), p. 1.
17. See Jones 1990, p. 267.
18. Helwig, Poulin and Powell 2007 (see note 14), p. 1.
19. Ibid., p. 13.
20. Ibid., p. 5.
21. Rebecca Ploeger, Canvas Samples (Report), 2005, Art Conservation Program, Queen's University.
22. Gus Shurvell, FTIR Analysis of Lining Adhesives from *A View of Gibraltar*, 2005, Art Conservation Program, Queen's University.
23. Gus Shurvell, FTIR Analysis of Surface Cleaning Swabs from *A View of Gibraltar*, 2005, Art Conservation Program, Queen's University.
24. Scumbling is a technique whereby a thin layer of slightly lighter, opaque paint is applied over a darker tone. It can create softness and also create an optically cooler effect.
25. A false colour image depicts a subject in colours that do not correspond to the true colours of the subject.

CATALOGUE

JOSEPH WRIGHT OF DERBY

DERBY 1734 – DERBY 1797

1.

A View of Gibraltar during the destruction of the Spanish Floating Batteries, on the 13th of September, 1782

1785
Oil on canvas
160.9 × 234.7 cm

Kingston, Agnes Etherington Art Centre, Queen's University
Purchase, gift of Alfred and Isabel Bader, 2001 (44-014)

PROVENANCE

Wakefield, John Milnes, by 1786.

London, Piccadilly, Egremont House, James Milnes (his cousin; d. 1806); sold London, Peter Coxe, 16 June 1806, no. 60, £71.8 to "Smith" [Thomas Vernon].

Liverpool and London, Thomas Vernon, in 1806.

Northampton, Overstone Park, Samuel Jones Loyd, 1st Baron Overstone (d. 1883), by 1849.

London, Harriet Loyd-Lindsay, Lady Wantage (d. 1920), by descent; sold London, Curtis and Henson (with remaining contents of Overstone Park), 31 January – 3 February 1921, no. 982 (painter unidentified).

New York, Ehrich Galleries, by 1923 (as by John Singleton Copley).

Chicago, the Honorable Nathaniel C. Sears, 1923–1924 (as by Copley).

Elgin IL, Laura Davidson Sears Academy of Fine Arts, gift of the Hon. Nathaniel C. Sears, 1924–1967 (as by Copley).

Milwaukee, Lenz Art Gallery, in partnership with Alfred Bader, 1967–1973 (as attributed to Copley).

Milwaukee, Milwaukee Art Center, purchased with a gift of the Charleston Foundation in memory of Miss Paula Uihlein, 1973 (M1973.1); de-accessioned 2001 (as attributed to Wright of Derby).

New York, Christie's East, 10 October 2001, no. 46 (as by a follower of Joseph Wright of Derby).

Kingston, Agnes Etherington Art Centre, Queen's University, purchase, gift of Alfred and Isabel Bader, 2001 (44-014).

LITERATURE

William Hayley. *Ode to Mr. Wright of Derby*. Chichester: Dennett Jaques, 1783, passim.

William Hayley. "Lines by Wm. Hayley, Esq. to Mr. Wright, of Derby, on his Picture of the Attack at Gibraltar." *The European Magazine* 7 (March 1785), p. 226.

Erasmus Darwin. *The Loves of the Plants*. London: J. Johnson, 1790, Canto 1, line 177, p. 20 ("From Calpè [i.e. Gibraltar] starts the intolerable flash.")

Obituary of Joseph Wright of Derby, in *The Kentish Weekly Post*. No. 1839 (8 September 1797), p. 63.

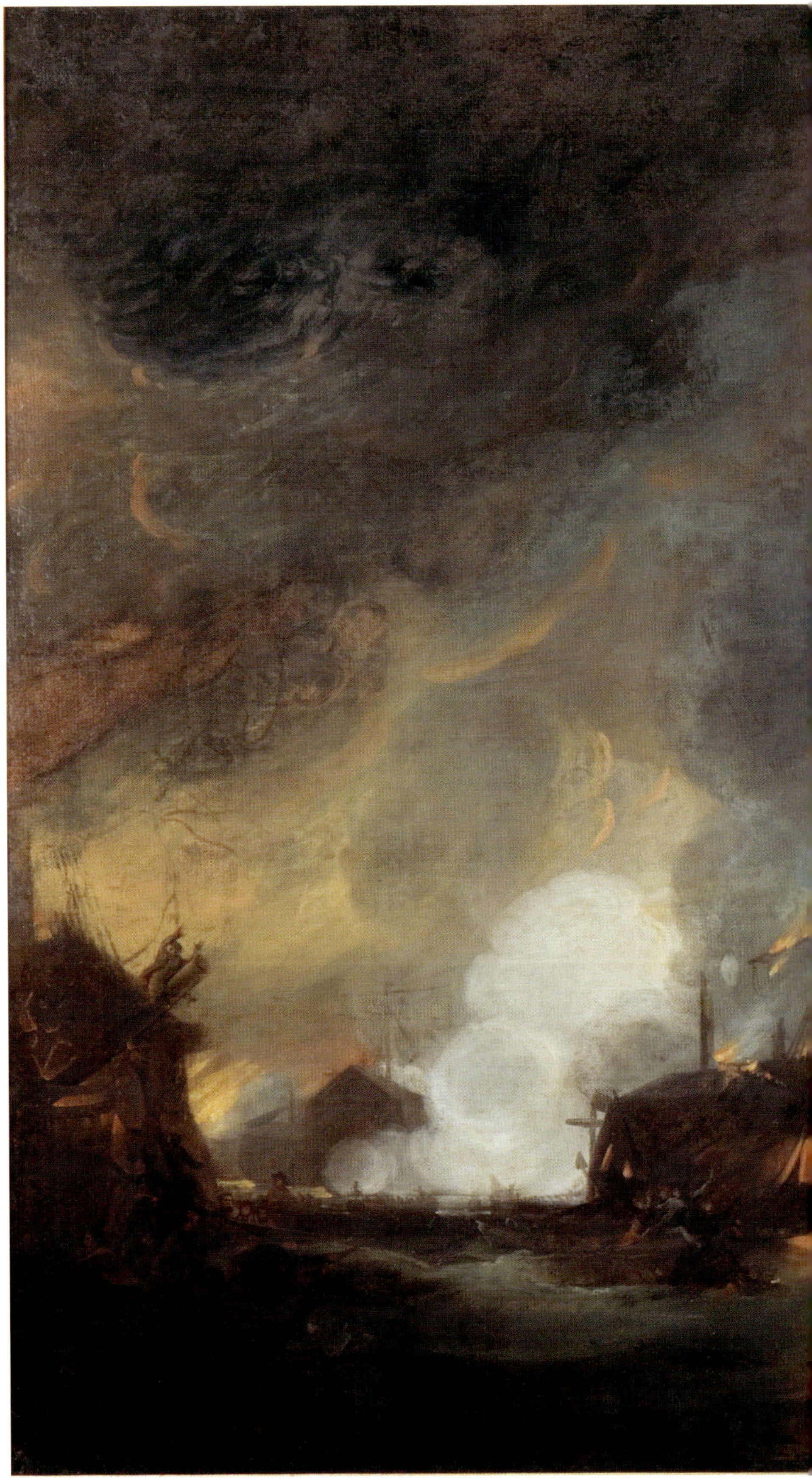

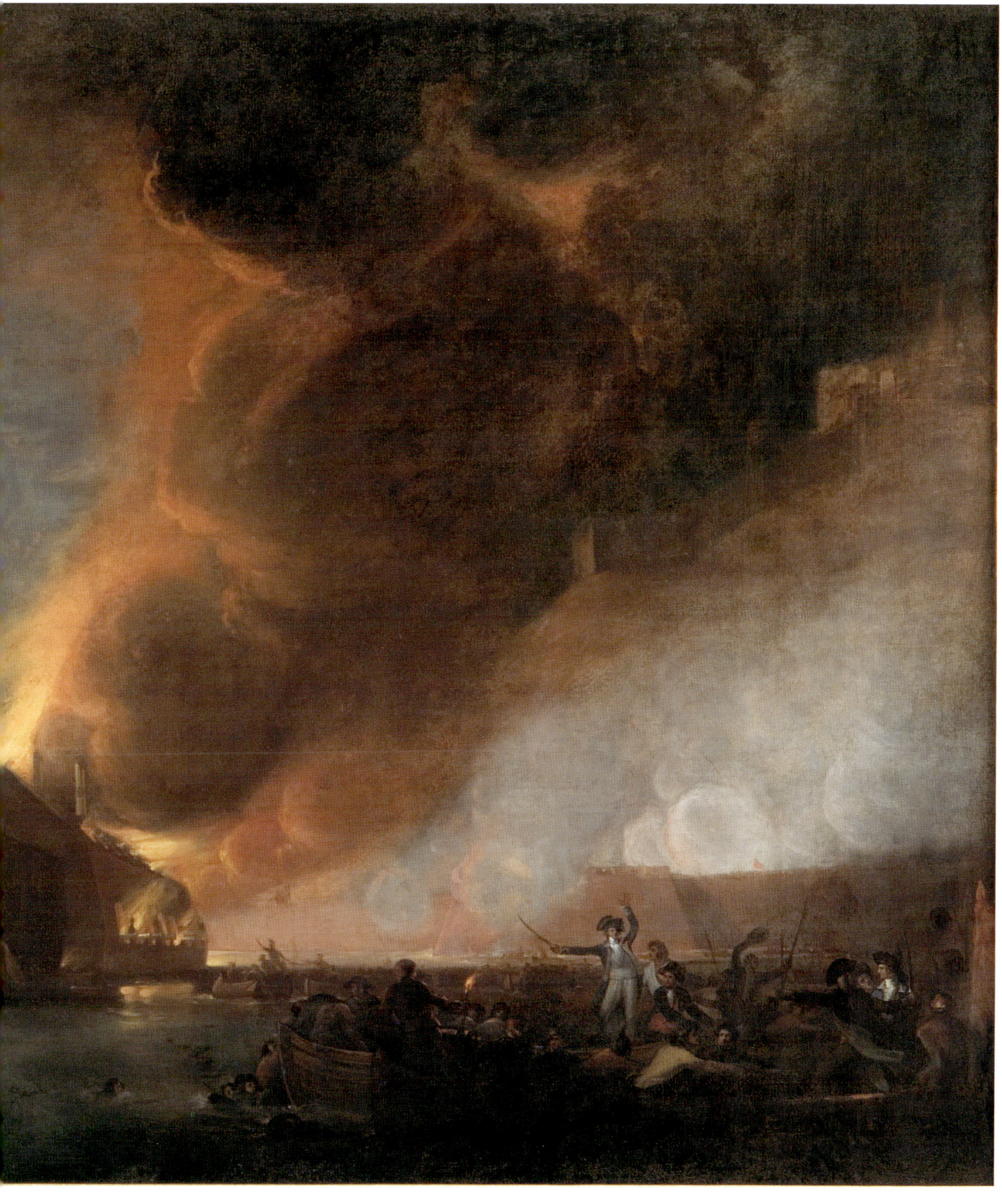

"Obituary of remarkable Persons; with Biographical Anecdotes." *Gentleman's Magazine* 67, part 3 (September 1797), p. 804 (as with J. Milnes, Esq. of Wakefield).

Rev. William Turner. "Observations on a tour through parts of York and Lancashire, read August 8th, 1797." In "Papers read at the Monthly Meetings, 1793–1814." Newcastle upon Tyne, Literary and Philosophical Society (N800/1), vol. 2; published by "V.F." in *The Monthly Magazine* 4 (September 1797), pp. 173–177.

"Memoirs of the Life of the Late Joseph Wright, Esq. of Derby, with a List of his Principal Paintings." *The Edinburgh Magazine of Literary Miscellany* (November 1797), p. 325.

"Biographical Register of eminent Persons deceased in 1797." *Universal Magazine of Knowledge and Pleasure* 102 (April 1798), p. 268.

"Wright of Derby." *The Penny Cyclopædia of the Society for the Diffusion of Useful Knowledge*, vol. 27. London: Charles Knight, 1843, p. 589.

"British Institution: Exhibition of Old Masters." (Review of: *Pictures by Italian, Spanish, Flemish, Dutch, French and English Masters* exhibition. London: British Institution, 1849). In *The Athenæum* 1131 (30 June 1849), p. 675.

"The Modern British Masters at Manchester." (Review of: *The Art Treasures of the United Kingdom* exhibition, Manchester, 1857). In *The Saturday Review* 3, no. 8 (27 June 1857), p. 595.

William Bemrose. "Wright of Derby. A Biographical Notice." *The Reliquary* 4 (1863–1864), pp. 210–212.

Llewellynn Jewitt. "Wright of Derby." *The Art-Journal* 60 (December 1866), p. 377.

John Piggot, Jr. "The Golden Age of Art." *The Art-Journal* (December 1871), p. 278.

Bradbury 1883, p. 595.

Bemrose 1885, pp. 23, 59–60, 74–76.

Algernon Graves. *A Century of Loan Exhibitions 1813–1912*, vol. 4. London: A. Graves, 1914, p. 1717.

Catalogue of the Laura Davidson Sears Academy of Fine Arts of the Elgin Academy and Junior College. Elgin, IL: Elgin Academy, 1924, pp. 8–9, no. 13 (as by Copley).

The Laura Davidson Sears Academy of Fine Arts of the Elgin Academy. Elgin, IL: Elgin Academy, 1938, no. 84 (as by Copley).

American Paintings from The Collection of the Laura Davidson Sears Academy of Fine Arts of the Elgin Academy, Elgin, Illinois. Milwaukee: Lenz Art Gallery, 1968, no. 11 (as by Copley).

Nicolson 1968, vol. 1, pp. 16, 131 note 7, 154, 159–60, 248 no. 245 (as lost).

Erdmann 1974, pp. 270–272 (as by Wright of Derby).

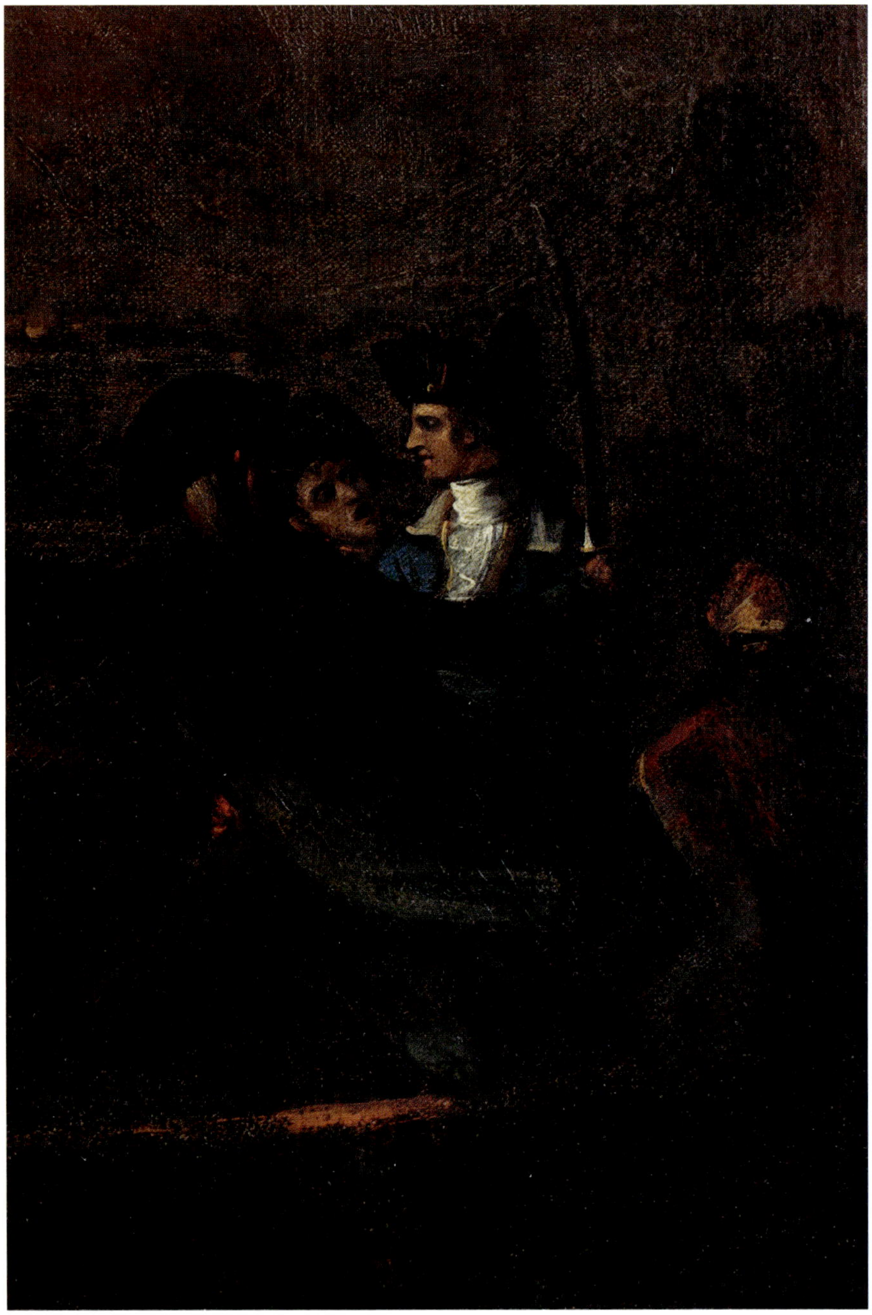

C. P. Darcy. *The Encouragement of the Fine Arts in Lancashire 1760–1860*. Remains Historical and Literary Connected with the Palatine Counties of Lancaster and Chester. Vol. 24, Third Series. Manchester: Manchester University Press for The Chetham Society, 1976, p. 139.

Richard Daniel Altick. *The Shows of London*. Cambridge, MA: Harvard University Press, 1978, p. 97.

Joseph Farington. *The Diary of Joseph Farington*, vol. 7. Kathryn Cave, ed. New Haven/London: Yale University Press, 1982, p. 2797 (entry for 26 June 1806).

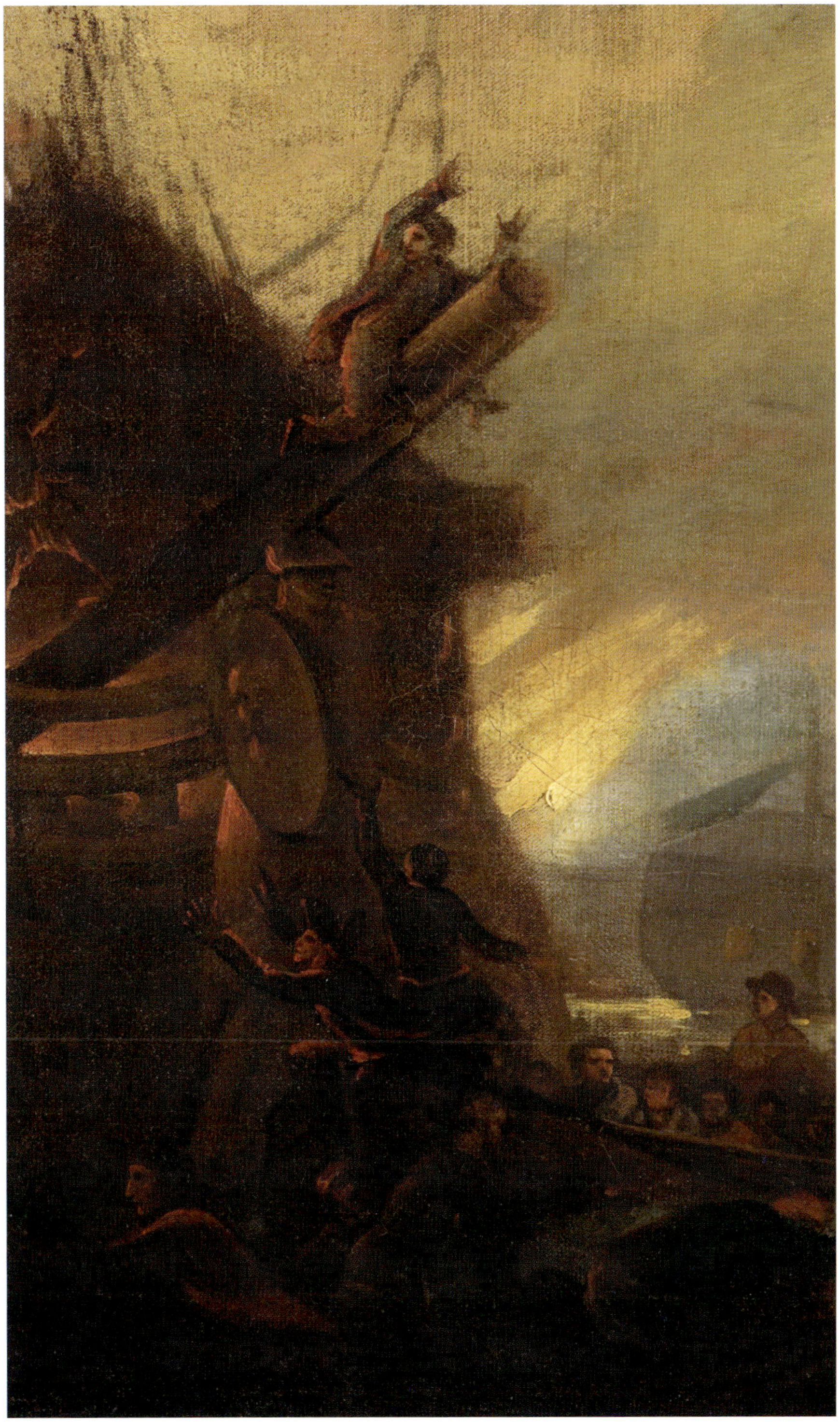

Helen A. Cooper. *John Trumbull: The Hand and Spirit of a Painter*. Exhibition catalogue. New Haven: Yale University Art Gallery, 1982, p. 62 note 11 (as by Wright of Derby).

Nicolson 1988, p. 745 (as by Wright of Derby).

Egerton 1990, pp. 69 (as "now widely thought to be not by Wright"), 134 (referring to the "now lost" painting).

Peter Harrington. *British Artists and War: The Face of Battle in Paintings and Prints, 1700–1914*. London and Mechanicsburg, PA: Greenhill Books and Stackpole Books, 1993, pp. 50, 342–343, no. 939.

John Chapple. *Elizabeth Gaskell: The Early Years*. Manchester/New York: Manchester University Press, 1997, p. 91.

Mark Hallett. "Painting." In Ian Calman et al., *An Oxford Companion to the Romantic Age*. New York/Oxford: Oxford University Press, 2001, p. 254.

Gert-Rudolf Flick. *Missing Masterpieces: Lost Works of Art 1450–1900*. London: British Art Journal, 2003, p. 7 (as by Wright, no longer missing).

Alfred Bader. "Lost Masterpieces and Happy Endings." *Queen's Quarterly* 114, no. 1 (Spring 2007), pp. 97–108.

Desmond King-Hele. *The Collected Letters of Erasmus Darwin*. Cambridge: Cambridge University Press, 2007, p. 238.

Bonehill 2008, pp. 521–544 (passim, as by Wright).

Barker 2009, pp. 3, 7 note 22 (as not by Wright), 40, 42, 58 notes 615 (as untraced, presumably destroyed) and 616, 59 note 692 (as *The Siege of Gibraltar*), 102 (Letter 45 note 3), 102–103 (Letter 46 note 2), 107 (Letter 50 note 2), 108 (Letter 53, as: "my fire"), 113 (Letter 60), 114 (Letter 61), 115–116 (Letter 63), 118 (Letters 67 and 68), 120 (Letter 71), 139 (Letter 106 note 4), 149 (Letter 122), 169 (extract from the *Memoir* of Hannah Wright, 1850, p. 111).

EXHIBITION CATALOGUES

Hayley 1785, p. 8, no. 24.

Pictures by Italian, Spanish, Flemish, Dutch, French and English Masters. London: British Institution, 1849, p. 13, no. 117.

Catalogue of the Art Treasures of the United Kingdom Collected at Manchester in 1857. London: Bradbury and Evans, 1857, p. 80, no. 81.

"The Siege of Gibraltar": An Art Historical Mystery Solved. Typescript. Milwaukee: Art History Gallery, University of Milwaukee-Wisconsin, 1973, no. 20.

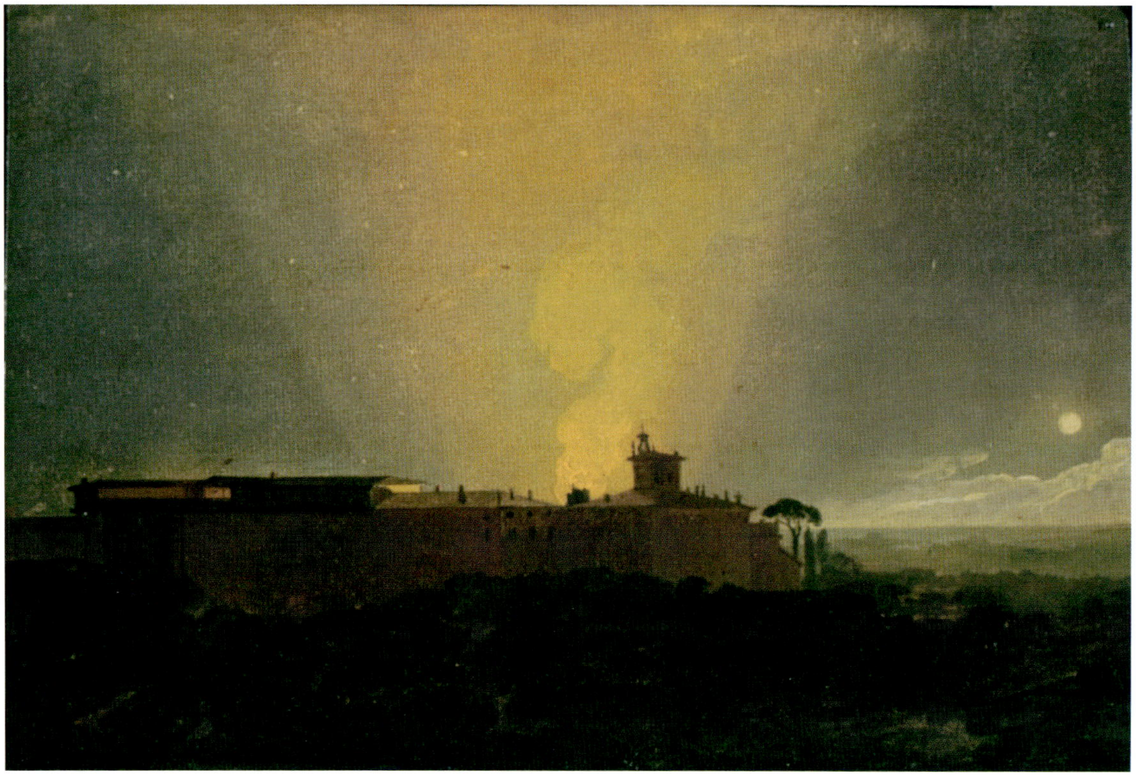

2.
Quirinale by Moonlight

Around 1790
Oil on paper, mounted on board
26.7 × 39.4 cm

Kingston, Agnes Etherington Art Centre, Queen's University
Purchase, Alfred and Isabel Bader and the Government of Canada, 1988 (31-005)

PROVENANCE

Ford Hall, Mansfield, Derbyshire, John Holland (d. 1807); by descent to his wife.

Left in trust to Joseph Bilbie (d. 1812), a relation of John Hall.

Mary Anne Bilbie (d. 1877), his daughter, who married Francis Hall of Park Hall.

Park Hall, Mansfield, Derbyshire, Francis Hall (d. 1928); nephew of Mary Anne Bilbie, son of her husband's younger brother Geoffrey Brock Hall of Park Hall; he moved to Guelph ON in 1914.

Riverslea, Guelph ON, Flora Caroline Hall (d. 1939); sold Toronto, Ward-Price Limited, 23–28 September 1946, no. 760 (as: *Fire and Sunset Landscape and Convent* [sic] *Near Rome*, oil on canvas, 12 × 16 ½ in. [30.5 × 40.6 cm]).

Hamilton ON, James Flinthoff.

London ON, Vancouver, Toronto and Ottawa, Prof. William Dale (purchased in 1957).

Kingston ON, Agnes Etherington Art Centre, Queen's University, purchase with the support of Alfred and Isabel Bader and the Government of Canada, 1988.

LITERATURE

Nicolson 1968, vol. 1, pp. 84 note 6, 138, 249, no. 248; vol. 2, p. 218 (pl. 348).

Deborah M. Brown. "A Question of Attribution: Eight British Landscape Paintings given to Joseph Wright of Derby (1734–1797) in the Queen's University Art Collection." M.A. thesis, Queen's University, 1990, passim.

EXHIBITION CATALOGUE

Egerton 1990, p. 196, no. 125 (as: *Fire at a Villa seen by Moonlight, probably in the Roman Campagna*, around 1774/75. Note: despite Egerton's objection, the motif represented here must be the Quirinale Palace: its silhouette and distinctive tower are rendered with accuracy. There is furthermore no reason to believe that Wright must have painted this scene on site during his Italian journey. He most likely worked it up from a drawing, in the later style that Nicolson observes).

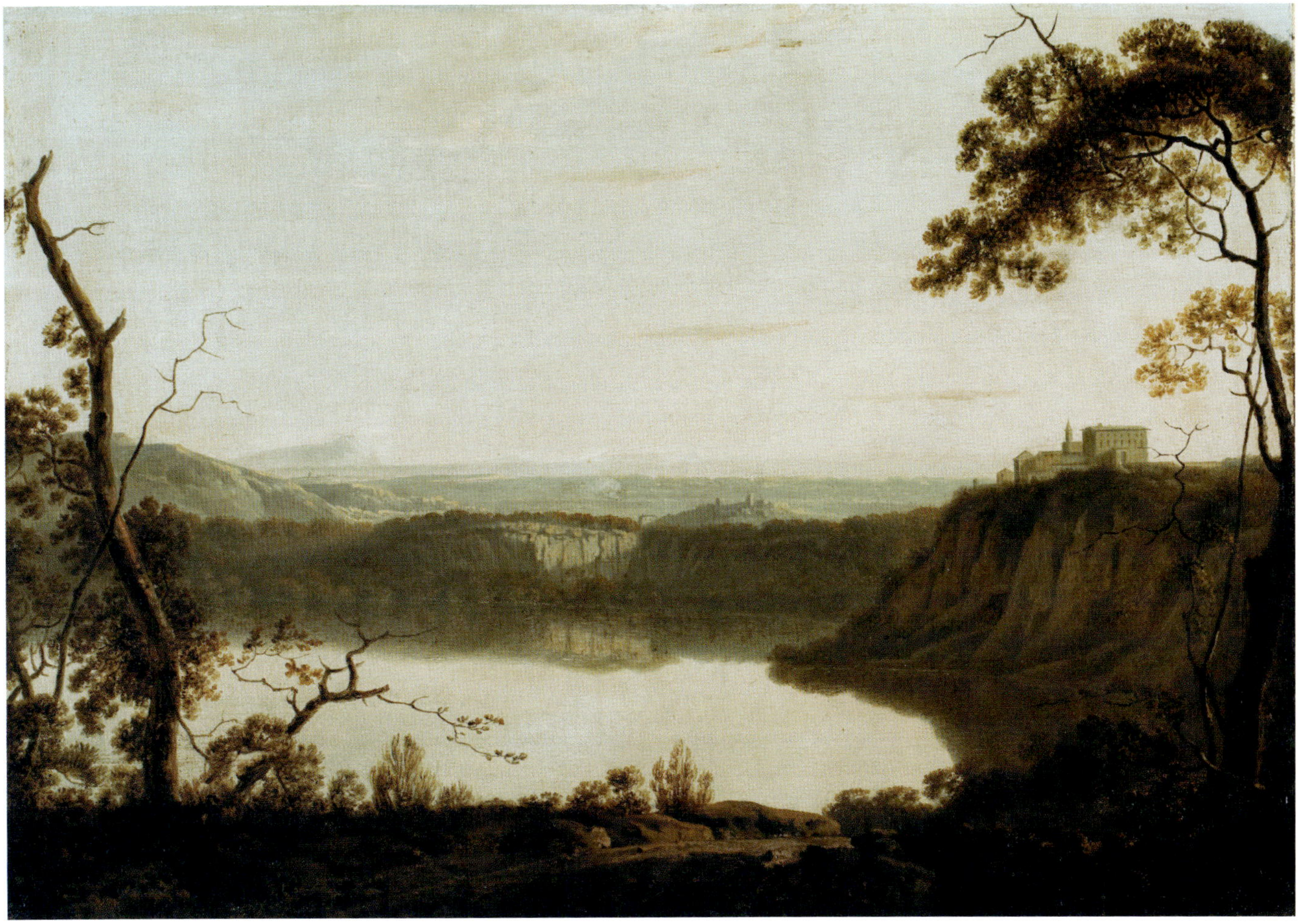

3.
Lake Nemi

Around 1790
Oil on canvas
43.2 × 60.8 cm

Kingston, Agnes Etherington Art Centre, Queen's University
Purchase, Alfred and Isabel Bader and the Government of Canada, 1988 (31-006)

PROVENANCE

See cat. 2; in Hall sale, no. 865 (as: *Gulf of Salerno* [sic], oil on canvas, 16 × 23 in. [40.6 × 58.4 cm], very fine; with note: "This picture was in the 1785 London exhibition" [sic]).

LITERATURE

Nicolson 1968, vol. 1, pp. 84, 137, 251, no. 256; vol. 2, pp. 201 (pl. 318).

Deborah M. Brown. "A Question of Attribution: Eight British Landscape Paintings given to Joseph Wright of Derby (1734–1797) in the Queen's University Art Collection." M.A. thesis, Queen's University, 1990, passim.

EXHIBITION CATALOGUE

Joseph Wright of Derby 1734–1797. New York: Durlacher Bros., 1960, no. 17.

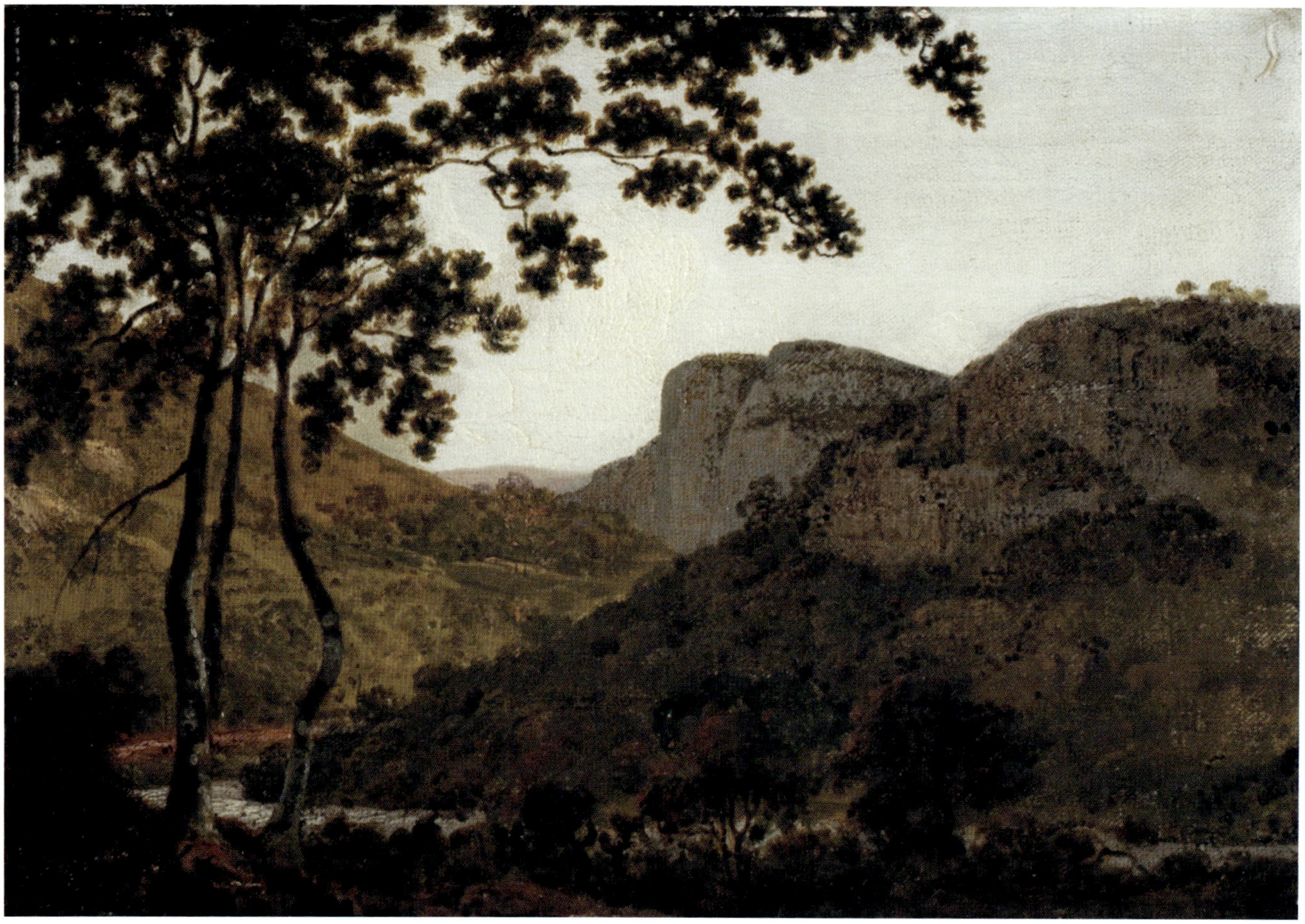

4.
Derwent Valley, Derbyshire

Around 1790
Oil on canvas
29.8 × 45 cm

Kingston, Agnes Etherington Art Centre, Queen's University
Purchase, Alfred and Isabel Bader and the Government of Canada, 1988 (31-007)

PROVENANCE

See cat. 2; in Hall sale, no. 766 (as: *Derbyshire Landscape and Hills*, oil on canvas, 12 × 16 ½ in. [30.4 × 41.9 cm], period frame).

LITERATURE

Nicolson 1968, vol. 1, pp. 89–90, 138, 262, no. 300; vol. 2, p. 196 (pl. 308).

Patricia R. Andrew. "A Landscape by Joseph Wright of Derby." *Burlington Magazine* 128, no. 1003 (October 1986), p. 743.

Deborah M. Brown. "A Question of Attribution: Eight British Landscape Paintings given to Joseph Wright of Derby (1734–1797) in the Queen's University Art Collection." M.A. thesis, Queen's University, 1990, passim.

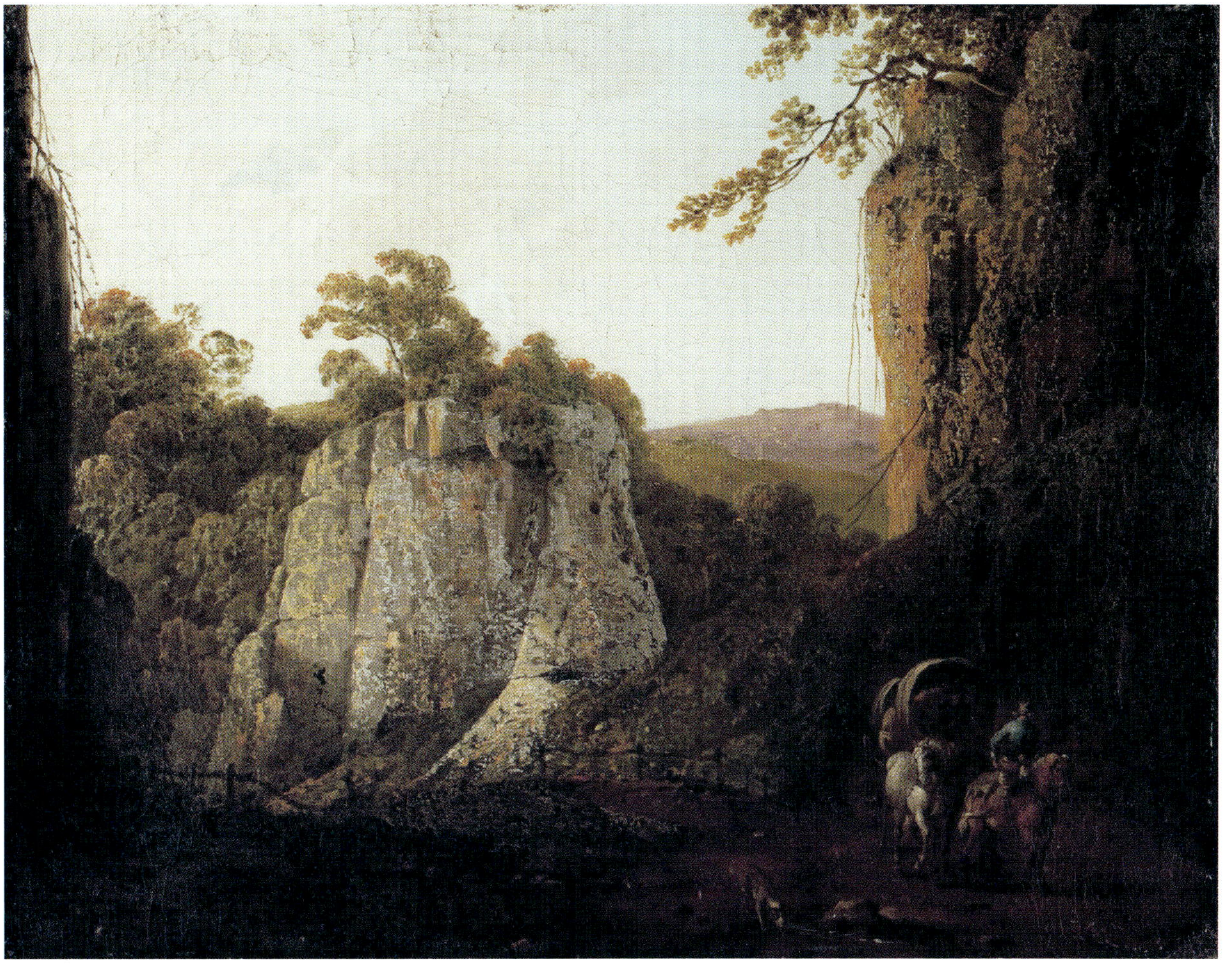

5.
Cut Through the Rock, Cromford

Around 1790
Oil on canvas
46 × 56.2 cm

Kingston, Agnes Etherington Art Centre, Queen's University
Purchase, Alfred and Isabel Bader and the Government of Canada, 1988 (31-008)

PROVENANCE

See cat. 2; in Hall sale, no. 756 (as: *The Cut Through the Rock at Crumford* [sic], oil on canvas, 18 ½ × 23 in. [47 × 58.4 cm], period frame).

LITERATURE

Nicolson 1968, vol. 1, pp. 90, 138, 167 (fig. 139), 265, no. 314; vol. 2, p. 210 (pl. 333).

Deborah M. Brown. "A Question of Attribution: Eight British Landscape Paintings given to Joseph Wright of Derby (1734–1797) in the Queen's University Art Collection." M.A. thesis, Queen's University, 1990, passim (as by Wright and an unknown artist).

Ian S. Hodkinson and Deborah M. Child. "An 18th-Century Artist-Applied Lining: Joseph Wright of Derby's *Cut Through the Rock at Cromford*." *Journal of the American Institute for Conservation* 34, no. 3 (1995), passim.

Barker 2009, pp. 43, 60 note 723.

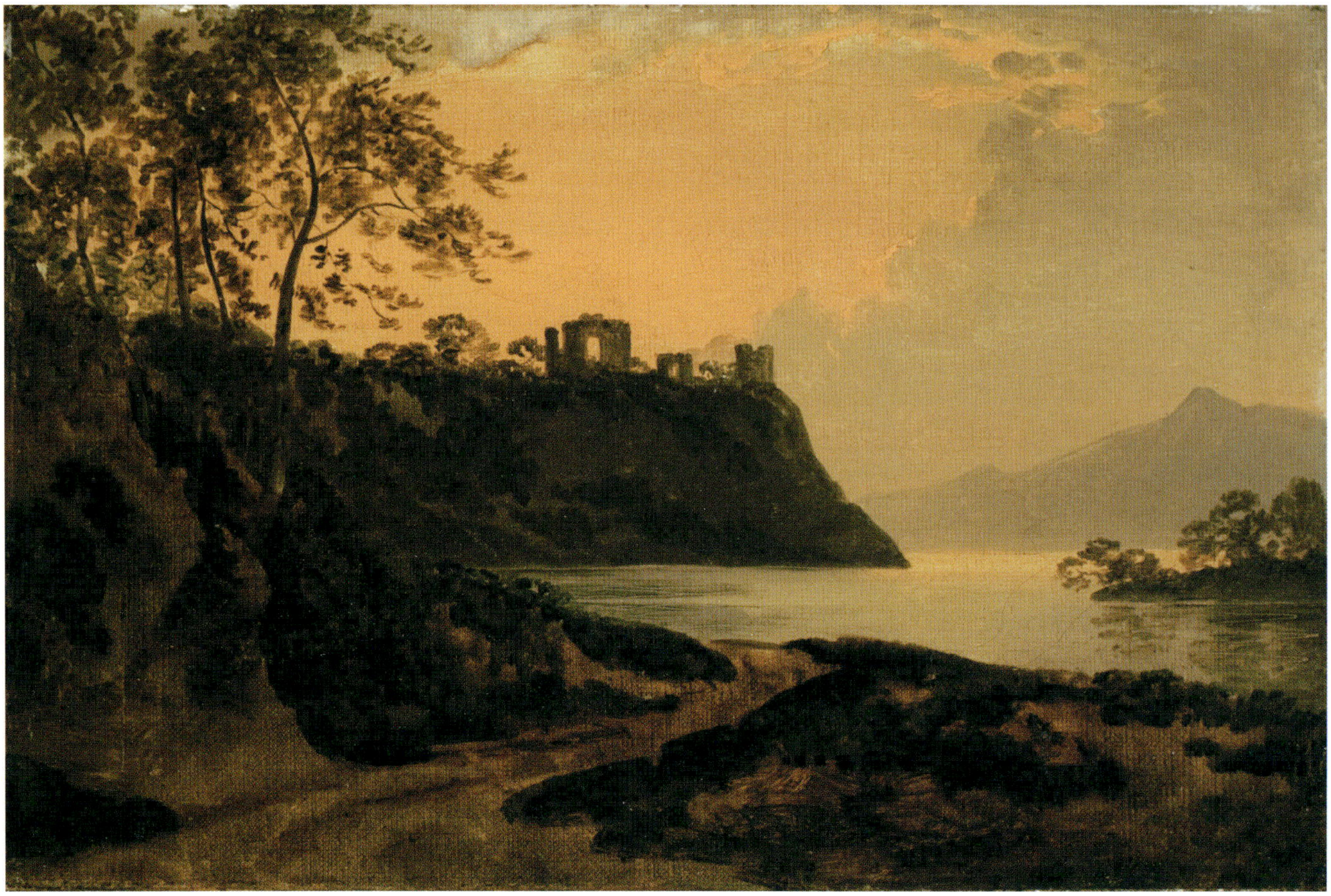

6.
Landscape with Ruined Castle

Around 1790
Oil on canvas
30.5 × 45.2 cm

Kingston, Agnes Etherington Art Centre, Queen's University
Purchase, Alfred and Isabel Bader and the Government of Canada, 1988 (31-009)

PROVENANCE

See cat. 2; in Hall sale, no. 762 (as: *Landscape with a Ruined Castle*, oil on canvas, 12 1/2 × 8 in. [31.7 × 20.3 cm]; sic: 18 in.).

LITERATURE

Nicolson 1968, vol. 1, pp. 93, 138, 269, no. 332; vol. 2, p. 218 (pl. 349).

Deborah M. Brown. "A Question of Attribution: Eight British Landscape Paintings given to Joseph Wright of Derby (1734–1797) in the Queen's University Art Collection." M.A. thesis, Queen's University, 1990, passim (as not by Wright).

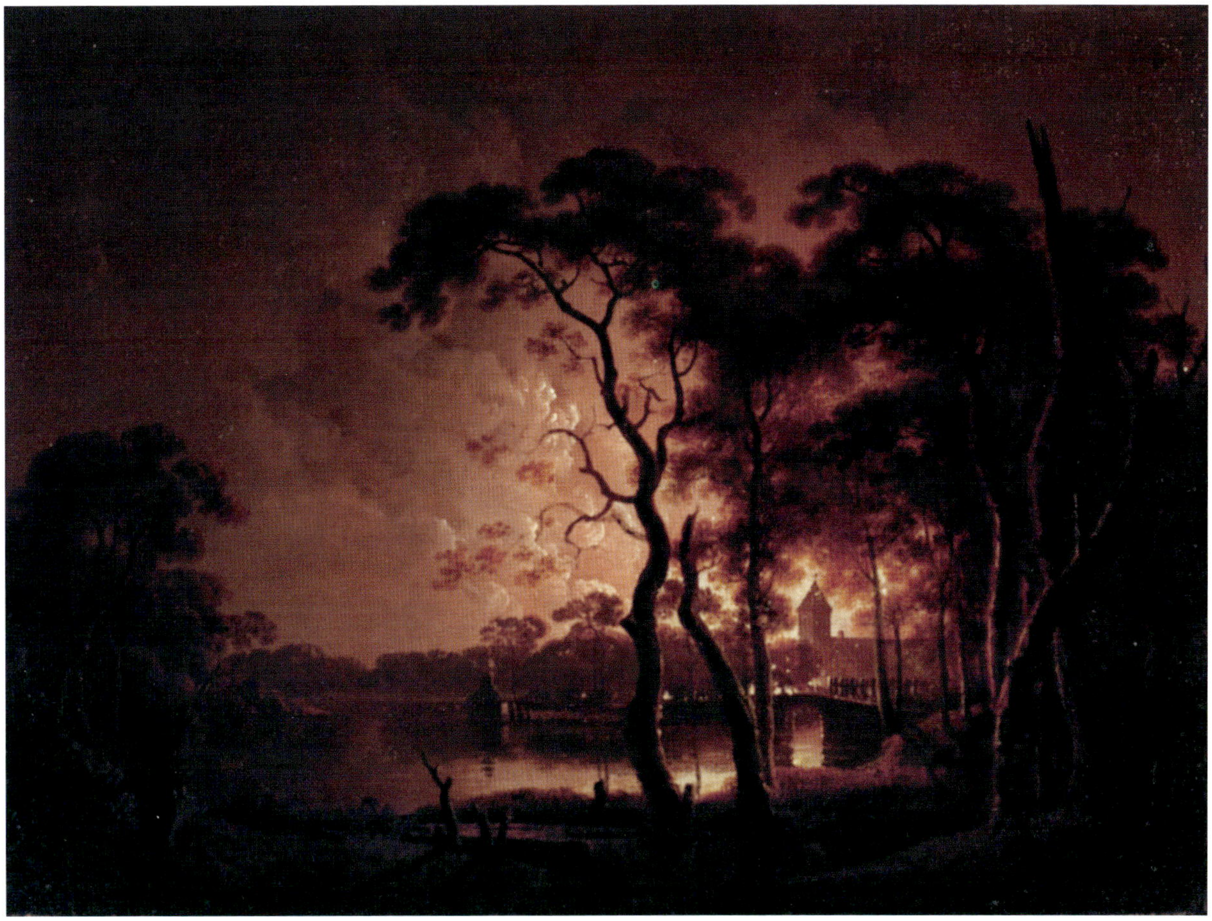

7.

Fire Seen Through Trees

Signed and dated lower right: I.W. Pt 1793
Oil on canvas
40.6 × 54.6 cm

Kingston, Agnes Etherington Art Centre, Queen's University
Purchase, Alfred and Isabel Bader and the Government of Canada, 1988 (31-010)

PROVENANCE

See cat. 2; in Hall sale, no. 761 (as: *Fire Scene, Trees and Water by Night*, oil on canvas, 16 × 21 1/4 in. [40.6 × 54 cm]).

LITERATURE

Nicolson 1968, vol. 1, pp. 92, 138, 270, no. 335; vol. 2, p. 210 (pl. 332).

Deborah M. Brown. "A Question of Attribution: Eight British Landscape Paintings given to Joseph Wright of Derby (1734–1797) in the Queen's University Art Collection." M.A. thesis, Queen's University, 1990, passim.

Barker 2009, pp. 33, 56 note 472.

EXHIBITION CATALOGUE

Joseph Wright of Derby 1734–1797. New York: Durlacher Bros., 1960, no. 26.

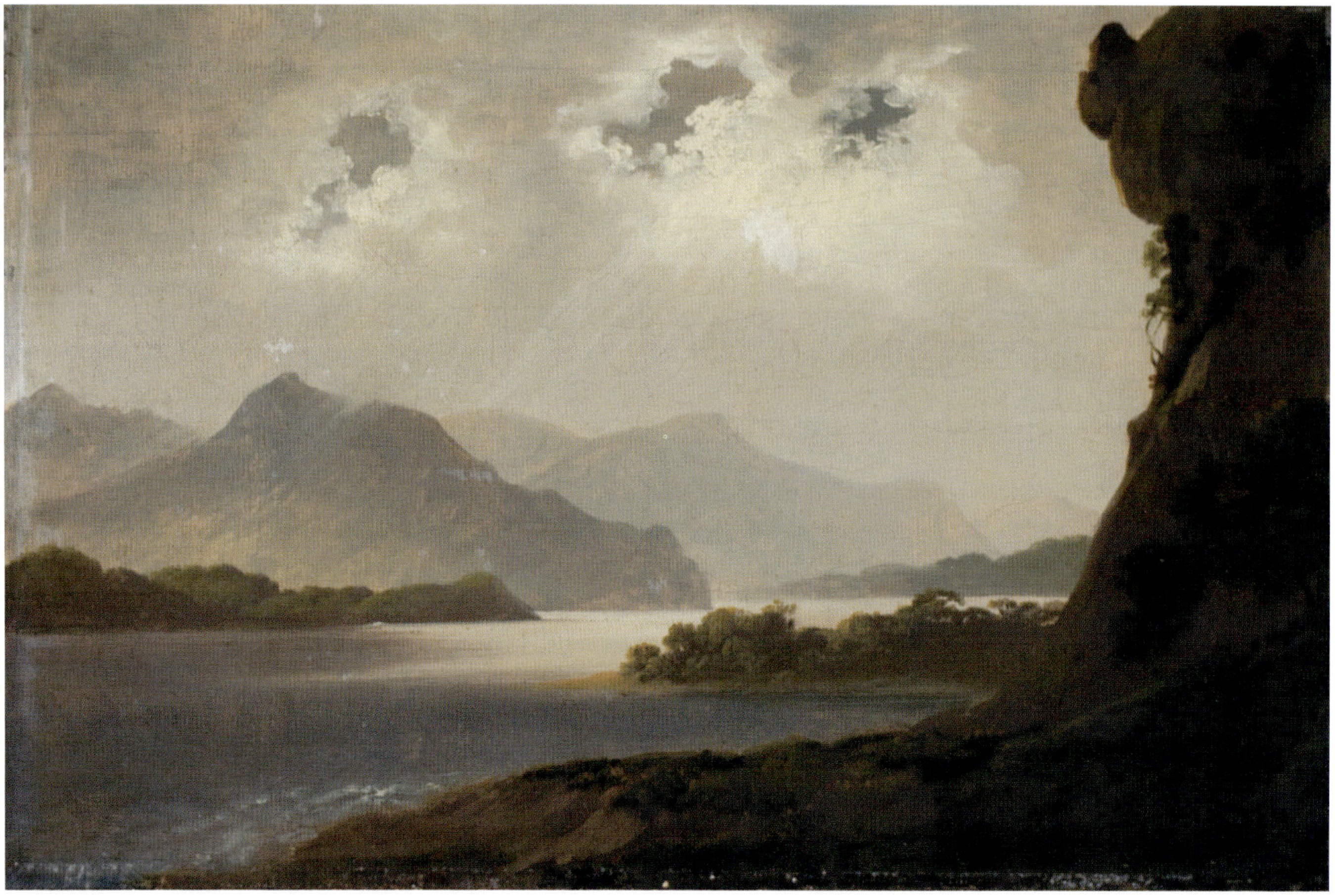

8.
Lake Landscape

Around 1790
Oil on canvas
31.1 × 46.3 cm

Kingston, Agnes Etherington Art Centre, Queen's University
Purchase, Alfred and Isabel Bader and the Government of Canada, 1988 (31-011)

PROVENANCE

See cat. 2; in Hall sale, no. 765 (as: *Landscape*, oil on canvas, 12 × 17 ½ in. [31.4 × 44.5 cm], very pleasant, period frame).

LITERATURE

Nicolson 1968, vol. 1, pp. 93, 138, 271, no. 339; vol. 2, p. 219 (pl. 350).

Deborah M. Brown. "A Question of Attribution: Eight British Landscape Paintings given to Joseph Wright of Derby (1734–1797) in the Queen's University Art Collection." M.A. thesis, Queen's University, 1990, passim (as not by Wright).

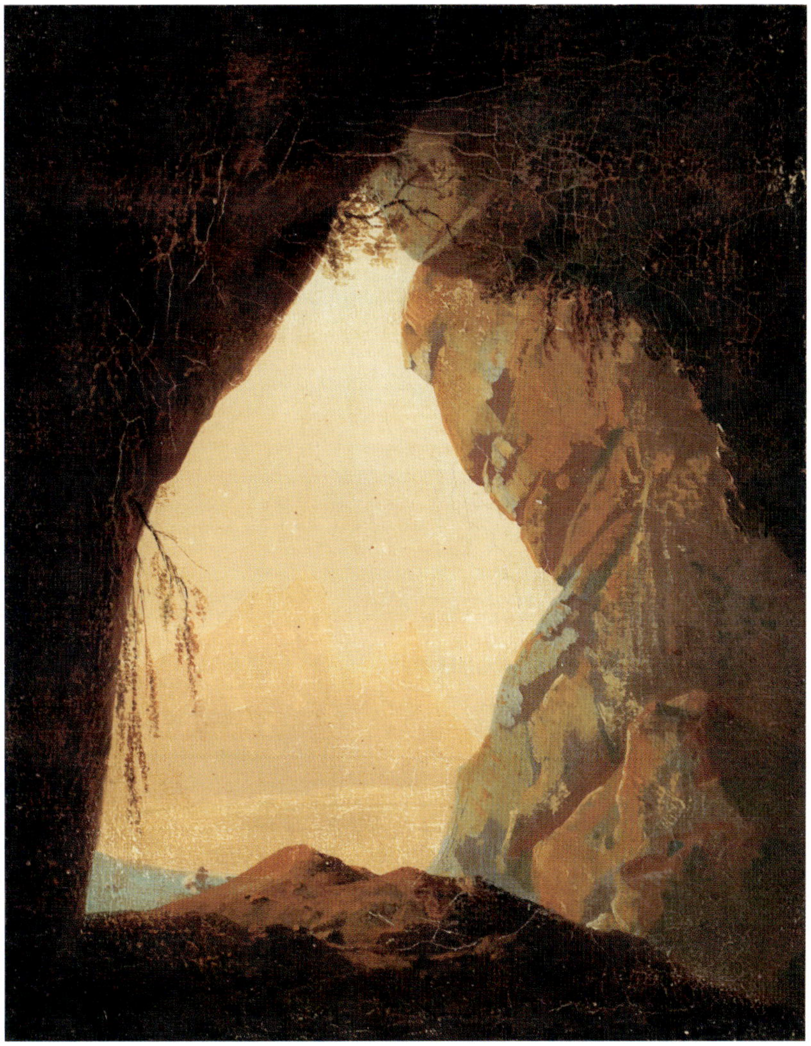

9.
Seashore through Arch

Around 1795
Oil on canvas
49.8 × 40 cm

Kingston, Agnes Etherington Art Centre, Queen's University
Purchase, Alfred and Isabel Bader and the Government of Canada, 1988 (31-012)

PROVENANCE

See cat. 2; in Hall sale, no. 757 (as: *Cleft in the Rock, Italian Cavern*, oil on canvas, 15 × 19 in. [38.1 × 48.2 cm], sic: 19 × 15 in., period frame).

LITERATURE

Nicolson 1968, vol. 1, p. 271, no. 340.

Deborah M. Brown. "A Question of Attribution: Eight British Landscape Paintings given to Joseph Wright of Derby (1734–1797) in the Queen's University Art Collection." M.A. thesis, Queen's University, 1990, passim.

Barker 2009, pp. 39, 58 note 553, 153 note 2.

EXHIBITION CATALOGUE

Joseph Wright of Derby 1734–1797. New York: Durlacher Bros., 1960, no. 14.

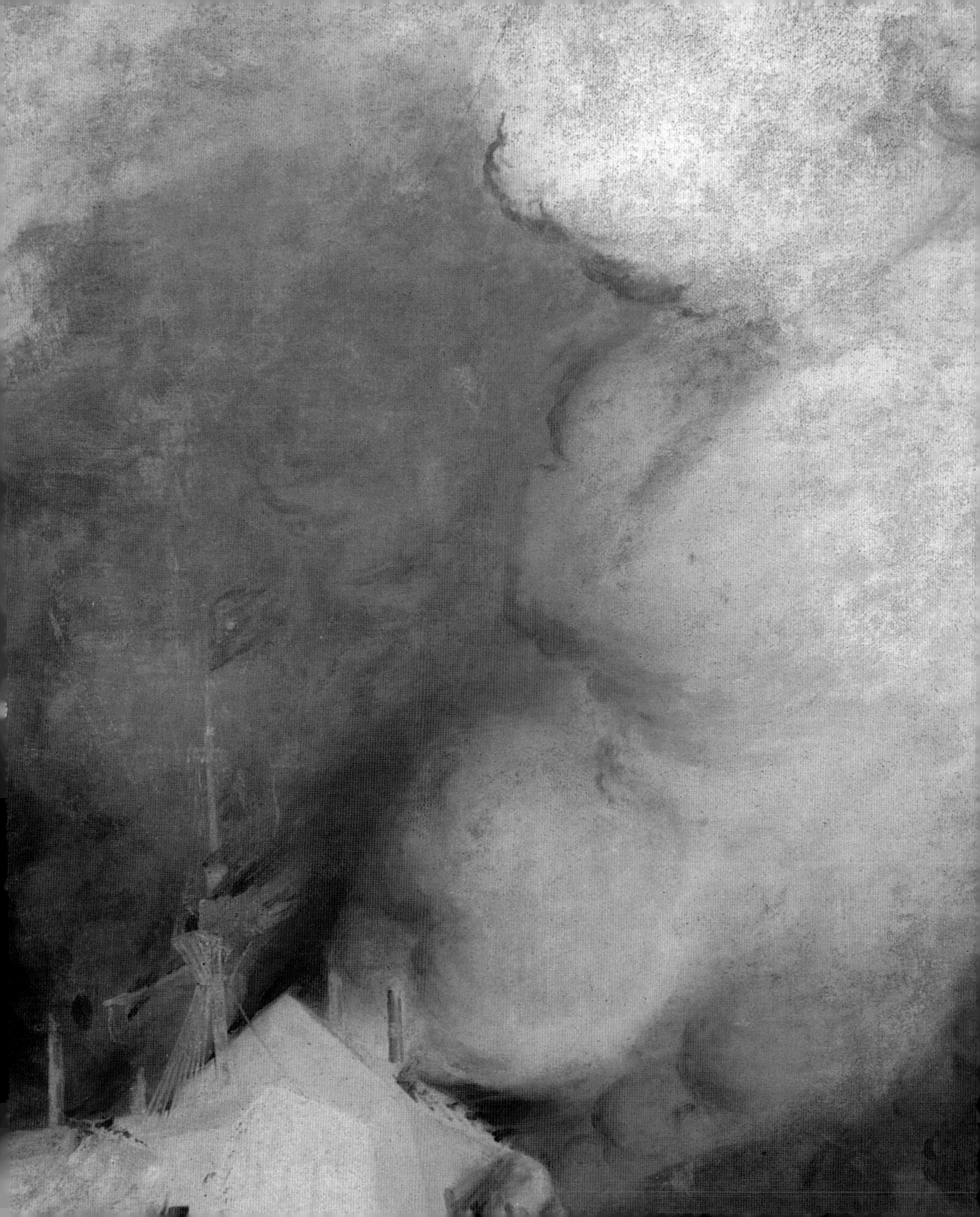